Lecture Notes in Computer Science 13238

More information about this series at https://link.springer.com/bookseries/558

Farid Karimipour · Sabine Storandt (Eds.)

Web and Wireless Geographical Information Systems

19th International Symposium, W2GIS 2022
Constance, Germany, April 28–29, 2022
Proceedings

Editors
Farid Karimipour 🆔
Institute of Science and Technology Austria
Klosterneuburg, Austria

Sabine Storandt
Universität Konstanz
Konstanz, Baden-Württemberg, Germany

ISSN 0302-9743   ISSN 1611-3349 (electronic)
Lecture Notes in Computer Science
ISBN 978-3-031-06244-5   ISBN 978-3-031-06245-2 (eBook)
https://doi.org/10.1007/978-3-031-06245-2

This Springer imprint is published by the registered company Springer Nature Switzerland AG
The registered company address is: Gewerbestrasse 11, 6330 Cham, Switzerland

Preface

Recent developments in wireless internet technologies have generated an increasing interest in the diffusion and processing of a large volume of geo-spatial information. Spatially enabled wireless and internet devices also offer new ways of accessing and analyzing this geo-referenced information in both real-world and virtual spaces. Consequently, new challenges and opportunities have appeared in the GIS research community.

These proceedings contain the papers selected for presentation at the 19th edition of the International Symposium on Web and Wireless Geographical Information Systems (W2GIS 2022) held in April 2022 and hosted by the University of Konstanz.

The symposium is intended to provide an up-to-date review of advances in both the theoretical and technical development of web and wireless geographical information systems. The 2022 edition was the 19th in a series of successful events, beginning with W2GIS 2001 in Kyoto and mainly alternating locations annually between East Asia and Europe.

W2GIS is organized as a full two-day symposium and provides an international forum for discussing advances in theoretical, technical, and practical issues in the field of wireless and internet technologies suited for the dissemination, usage, and processing of geo-referenced data.

This year, the submissions process attracted papers from almost all continents, demonstrating not only the growing importance of this field for researchers but also the growing impact these developments have on the daily lives of all citizens.

Each paper received at least three reviews and was ranked accordingly. The 13 accepted papers are all of excellent quality and cover topics such as web technologies and techniques, paths and navigation, movement analysis, web visualization, and novel applications.

We wish to thank the authors who contributed to this workshop for the high quality of their papers and presentations and their support of Springer LNCS. We would also like to thank the Program Committee for the quality and timeliness of their evaluations.

Finally, many thanks to the Steering Committee for providing continuous advice and recommendations.

April 2022

Farid Karimipour
Sabine Storandt

Organization

General Chairs

Farid Karimipour   Institute of Science and Technology Austria (ISTA), Austria

Sabine Storandt   University of Konstanz, Germany

Steering Committee

Michela Bertolotto   University College Dublin, Ireland
Christophe Claramunt   Naval Academy Research Institute, France
Sergio di Martino   University of Naples Federico II, Italy
Jérôme Gensel   University of Grenoble, France
Farid Karimipour   Institute of Science and Technology Austria (ISTA), Austria
Miguel R. Luaces   University of A Coruña, Spain
Sabine Storandt   University of Konstanz, Germany
Kazutoshi Sumiya   Kwansei Gakuin University, Japan
Martin Tomko   University of Melbourne, Australia

Program Committee

Daisuke Kitayama   Kogakuin University, Japan
Shiori Sasaki   Keio University, Japan
Feng Lu   Institute of Geographic Sciences and Natural Resources, China
Taro Tezuka   University of Tsukuba, Japan
Michela Bertolotto   University College Dublin, Ireland
Stephan Winter   University of Melbourne, Australia
Zhuqing Zhu   Wuhan University, China
Yuanyuan Wang   Yamaguchi University, Japan
Jérôme Gensel   University of Grenoble, France
Miguel R. Luaces   University of A Coruña, Spain
Alain Bouju   La Rochelle University, France
Songnian Li   Ryerson University, Canada
Xiang Li   ECNU, China
Kyoung-Sook Kim   AIST, Japan
Gavin McArdle   University College Dublin, Ireland

Contents

Multiple Views Extraction from Semantic Trajectories

Hassan Noureddine$^{(\boxtimes)}$, Cyril Ray, and Christophe Claramunt

Naval Academy Research Institute, Brest, France
{hassan.noureddine,cyril.ray,christophe.claramunt}@ecole-navale.fr

Abstract. The interest in exploiting crowd-sourced location information has recently emerged as it can bring many valuable benefits. This is particularly the case where multi-dimensional semantic information represent human trajectories and contextual information arising in indoor and outdoor spaces. Users have different interests when interpreting and analysing trajectories. While some users just want to visualise the data, others require either higher-level information or aggregated knowledge. This paper introduces a modelling approach and data manipulation mechanisms that extract from generic semantic trajectories multiple views at different levels of abstraction to produce hybrid spatial representation for mobility patterns. This approach considers a multi-layered graph representation for trajectories according to some given spatio-temporal, contextual and user-defined criteria. The approach has been experimented with real data and implemented within a graph database that illustrates its potential.

Keywords: Mobility data management · Semantic trajectories · Graph database

1 Introduction

The widespread adoption of mobile devices and connected sensors provides many opportunities to develop location-based services that homogeneously cover indoor and outdoor spaces. However, common modelling efforts are generally oriented towards either outdoor [15] or indoor spaces [9]. Moreover, it clearly appears that indoor and outdoor spaces, when associated in a unified modelling framework, should also consider different levels of granularity and abstraction to provide sufficient flexibility at the data manipulation level [6]. This will favour the emergence of a hierarchy of space that supports micro to macro data representations and manipulations. This might be of interest for many urban applications in which human movements should be manipulated throughout indoor and outdoor spaces. This is, for instance, the case when human mobility patterns are analysed throughout a series of trajectories that cover daily patterns from/to some places of interest and where additional contextual information can be appropriately considered.

© Springer Nature Switzerland AG 2022
F. Karimipour and S. Storandt (Eds.): W2GIS 2022, LNCS 13238, pp. 1–17, 2022.
https://doi.org/10.1007/978-3-031-06245-2_1

Exploring crowd-sourced location data and associated contextual information at a large scale should help to reveal mobility patterns and outliers, this being of benefit for many urban planning tasks using a holistic view in which human mobility should be considered in both indoor and outdoor spaces [13]. Such a holistic view can be represented by a generic multi-dimensional approach for modelling mobility patterns emerging in both spaces and where trajectories are continuous. There is a wide range of interests among users looking forward to multi-dimensional approaches for manipulating trajectories emerging in indoor and outdoor spaces. While some might be interested in a straight visualisation of these trajectories, others might either analyse trajectory patterns at the macro level or aggregated views depending on their interests. Such a generic approach should be flexible enough to represent these trajectories at different levels of granularity and different views. This raises the need for an abstract and hybrid representation that considers indoor and outdoor spaces at different levels of granularity and with a hierarchical and semantic representation.

In a previous work, we introduced a preliminary model for extracting multiple views of semantic trajectories according to users' interests [14]. In the present paper, we first develop a formal and logical extension of our previous work by developing data manipulation mechanisms for extracting semantic trajectories at different levels of abstraction according to different spatial and contextual user interests. The whole approach has been implemented on top of the Neo4j database and Cypher query language. An experimental validation using a real large set of contextual urban trajectories has been performed. The main contribution of this paper is a flexible view approach of semantic trajectories which is built upon an indoor/outdoor temporal hierarchy where places are considered as reference abstractions. The interest of the whole model is exemplified by a series of graph-based processing operations and performance evaluations that show its flexibility when implemented on top of a real data context. The whole framework is applied and experimented within the context of Polluscope project (polluscope.uvsq.fr), where human trajectories with multiple contextual data are collected in an environmental crowd-sensing context. The remainder of this paper is organised as follows. Section 2 discusses related work while Sect. 3 gives the modelling background for the representation of spatial and semantic trajectories. Section 4 introduces the multiple views of semantic trajectories. Section 5 evaluates the approach, while Sect. 6 concludes the paper and outlines some perspectives.

2   Related Work

Semantic-based representations of human trajectories have been addressed over the last years at the database and semantic levels. Regarding semantic approaches, Parent et al. [15] gives a survey on the representation of semantic trajectories with a focus on semantic approaches and stop and move abstractions. Stops and moves abstractions have been firstly introduced by Alvares et al. [1] and Spaccapietra et al. [17] in order to provide an appropriate semantic view of the data that supports valuable data manipulation and also reduce query complexity at the computational level. Several recent works have extended the semantic representation of trajectories by considering predefined criteria and in order to provide further trajectory data analysis [2]. Fileto et al. [4] introduced a framework to fill the gap between movement data and formal semantics. These authors provided an ontological model for semantic enrichment. Zheni et al. [18] developed a spatio-temporal abstract data type to encapsulate the spatial, temporal and semantics associated to a given trajectory. More recently, Mello et al. [11] extended the work in [2,4] towards multiple aspect trajectory sequences to support trajectories with any type of annotation. Cayèré et al. [3] considered multi-level and multiple aspect features to link semantics to trajectories. Ilarri et al. [6] raised the need for a representation of semantic trajectories at different levels of abstraction. Accordingly, it should be possible to commute from one given semantic to another one given some query requirements. Similarly, Pelekis et al. [16] developed a stop and move trajectory model to support different scales and spatio-temporal granularities. Kontarinis et al. [9] designed a specific semantic trajectory model for a museum case study that considers a hierarchical indoor spatial model. Jin and Claramunt [8] introduced a database management approach for representing and analysing human trajectories in an urban environment. Izquierdo et al. [7] introduced key-word expressions over semantic trajectories to search for individual stops and moves sequences. Our recent work [12,13] presented the main principles of a hierarchical multi-dimensional semantic trajectory modelling approach for trajectories evolving in indoor and outdoor spaces.

3   Background

Spatial Model. The assumptions made to represent human mobility emerging in indoor and outdoor spaces are to provide (1) a unified indoor and outdoor spatial model oriented to the representation of semantic trajectories, and where the specific spatial characteristics of indoor and outdoor spaces are taken into account, (2) to consider a flexible representation at different levels of abstraction and within a hierarchy of space and (3) to take into account the places where the mobility occurs and some points of interest (POI).

Let us first consider an indoor space $\mathbb{I}$ made up of a set LI of hierarchically ordering of nested indoor spatial layers. Similarly, an outdoor space $\mathbb{O}$ is made up of a set LO of hierarchically ordering of nested outdoor spatial layers. Let us define a reference space as follows:

$$\mathbb{S} = \mathbb{I} \cup \mathbb{O} \tag{1}$$

where $\mathbb{S}$ denotes the entire space encapsulating indoor and outdoor spaces and the embedding layers. Moreover, and in order to secure the connection and continuity between indoor and outdoor spaces, we define a constraint that guarantees that there should exist at least one layer L such as $L \in LO$ and $L \in LI$. As outdoor and indoor spaces are defined at complementary levels of abstraction and scale, let L denote the finest layer of outdoor space and the coarser layer of indoor space (e.g., Fig. 1 'building' layer). Overall, these layers represent the successive levels of abstraction and describe the spatial hierarchy embedded within the different indoor and outdoor layers (Fig. 1).

The modelling approach is materialised as a *place-based* representation where each *place* represents a location of interest in space, either indoor or outdoor, and located in a layer. Places are characterised by a list of spatial and thematic properties and their 'location' in the spatial hierarchy. This spatial hierarchy denotes the different levels of abstraction considered for the outdoor and indoor spaces (e.g., state, county, town, road, building; and building, floor, room, for outdoor and indoor spaces, respectively).

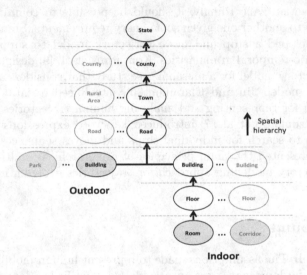

Fig. 1. Spatial model showing the hierarchical relationships between indoor and outdoor spatial layers.

A graph-based representation is defined for $\mathbb{S}$ as a multi-layered graph $G = (V, E)$ where $V = \bigcup\limits_{i=1}^{k} S_i \in \mathbb{L}$ and $E = \bigcup\limits_{i=1}^{n} E_i$ where E_i denotes the edges embedding the hierarchy over the indoor and outdoor layers S_i for $k, n \in \mathbb{N}$ (Fig. 1).

This spatial representation further supports a homogeneous representation of semantic trajectories in indoor and outdoor spaces at the manipulation level, and whose objective is to define the complete spatial environment where human mobility takes place. On top of this model, users can define POIs that might take place at any granularity in the model.

Semantic Trajectory Representation. The semantic trajectory representation should support the derivation of different trajectories according to either spatial (i.e., from micro to macro levels) or contextual properties (e.g., weather conditions, pollution exposition along a path) associated with raw trajectory data.

Let us first define T_{start} and T_{end} as time instants sets, and $[t_s, t_e]$ a time interval where $t_s \in T_{start}$, $t_e \in T_{end}$ and $t_e \leq t_s$. Next, a human trajectory can be associated to a sequence of places over a sequence of time intervals ($[t_s, t_e]$, $place$). This means that such a trajectory passes through a $place$ at a start time t_s and left it at an end time t_e. Similarly, we define a sequence of some given contextual attributes over a sequence of time intervals ($[t_s, t_e]$, $value$) for each context (e.g., NO_2) denoted by $c_i \in C$ where $value$ is its qualitative value that holds during $[t_s, t_e]$ and C is a set of crowd-sourced contexts. Finally, a semantic trajectory $semTraj_{id}$ is defined as a sequence of semantic trajectory segments. A semantic trajectory segment $\{[t_s, t_e], Sem\}$ denotes a homogeneous part of a trajectory valid over a time interval $[t_s, t_e]$ and for some contextual semantics where a list of semantic values Sem holds. A semantic trajectory is defined as:

$$semTraj_{id} = \{([t_{s1}, t_{e1}], Sem_1), ([t_{s2}, t_{e2}], Sem_2), ..., ([t_{sn}, t_{en}], Sem_n)\} \quad (2)$$

where $Sem_i = \{space : place_i, CS_i\}$ denotes a set of integrated spatial ($place_i$) and contextual semantics (CS_i) valid over a given time interval $[t_{si}, t_{ei}]$ with $t_{ei} < t_{si+1}$. $place_i$ belongs to the finest layer in $\mathbb{S}$ either indoor or outdoor and CS_i is a set of contextual semantics/dimensions ($NO_2 : value_{NO_2}; humidity : value_{humidity}; etc..$).

Overall, a semantic trajectory is defined as a sequence of annotated time intervals associated with spatial semantics embedded in the indoor and outdoor hierarchical spatial representations. A semantic trajectory represents an individual's continuous movement while integrating some contextual data that can be derived from the environment.

Since graphs are fundamental structures that provide an intuitive abstraction for modelling, interconnected and analysing complex data, we design/manage the semantic trajectory model as a path graph $P_{ST} = (V_{ST}, E_{ST})$ where V_{ST} denotes places embedded in the hierarchical spatial model associated to contextual semantic values and time intervals, while E_{ST} denotes edges that, on the one hand, link temporal, contextual and spatial semantics, and on the other hand link a trajectory segment to the next one; this denotes a movement to a state upon at least one semantic value change.

4   Multiple Views of Semantic Trajectories

Different levels of abstraction should be considered to provide a flexible enough representation of crowd-sourced semantic trajectories that continuously arise in indoor and outdoor spaces. This should facilitate the derivation of different points of view and interpretations, from micro to macro levels. We develop a derivation view mechanism that extracts, from a generic semantic trajectory, different flexible views derived from the spatial, temporal and contextual semantics. This concept of view is defined as a function:

$$SemTrajView: semTraj_{id} \times UserInterests \rightarrow viewTraj_{id}$$

where $UserInterests$ denotes a set of spatial and/or contextual semantics preferences/criteria and is given as:

$$UserInterests = \{Spatial : Layer, Contextual : Semantic\} \qquad (3)$$

where $Spatial$ denotes set of layers ($Layer$) and $Contextual$ the associated set of semantics ($Semantic$). For example, $UserInterests$ can denote some specific layers (e.g., Town, Road), or/and a semantic value of a contextual dimension (e.g., NO_2).

$viewTraj$ denotes some data extracted from $semTraj$ according to some $UserInterests$. We derive two types of views that are a hybrid representation based on either spatial or contextual criteria. The semantic trajectory is a generic representation, while the hybrid semantic trajectory is based on places of interests and the contextual-based semantic trajectory on a context of interest.

Hybrid Trajectory Representation. Place-based locations are linked to their hierarchical layers, this favouring the specification of a given trajectory at different levels of abstraction and of the hierarchy. For instance, when a user is interested in a finer spatial granularity for some contextual criteria of interests and coarser spatial granularity for others (or vice versa), the previous semantic trajectory is still a flat-like representation of the trajectory and do not provide such flexibility. For that purpose, the semantic trajectory representation is extended by a hybrid semantic trajectory concept whose purpose is to extract from a flat-like representation a hybrid one.

The hybrid semantic trajectory can be expressed at either homogeneous or heterogeneous levels of granularity and according to the user needs. The idea is to provide a flexible representation of the semantics associated with a human trajectory according to different application needs and user interests. A hybrid semantic trajectory is denoted by:

$$hybTraj_{id} = \{([t_{s1}, t_{e1}], place_1, CS_1), ([t_{s2}, t_{e2}], place_2, CS_2), ..., ([t_{sn}, t_{en}], place_n, CS_n)\} \qquad (4)$$

where $place_i$ belongs to a layer $L \in \mathbb{S}$ either in indoor or outdoor spaces and CS_i is a set of semantic values that hold during $[t_{si}, t_{ei}]$ with $t_{ei} < t_{si+1}$. $place_i$ represents a spatial place of interest that is an instance of a given layer of interest. For example, $place_i$ can be a floor or a town instance that belongs to the 'floor' or 'town' layers of the indoor or outdoor space, respectively. Therefore, POIs can be expressed at different levels of granularity and abstraction.

For example, at a coarse level of granularity, a human trajectory can be represented from a $town \in L_{Town}$ to another town and at a fine level from a $room \in L_{Room}$ to another room in indoor and from a road or building to another road or building in outdoor. Such layers are chosen according to the users' interests.

The main difference between *hybTraj* and *semTraj* is that *place* in *semTraj* belongs to the finest layer of granularity in the spatial model, and this for either indoor or outdoor spaces, although in *hybTraj* can belong to any layer of the spatial model.

Furthermore, users' interests are expressed by some criteria of interest, and where the layer granularity can be adjusted accordingly. Contextual values or spatial categories can be defined accordingly by the hybrid representation. For example, a contextual value and user interest can be {*temperature : hot*} and a spatial category and user interest can be {*category : restaurant*}.

According to the user interests, the hybrid semantic trajectory considers one spatial layer for its POIs when one of the user interests is available and a second spatial layer when none of the user interests is valid. In other words, given a level of reference, which is the finer one, it searches for a specified spatial granularity when one of the user interests is valid and another specified spatial granularity when there are no valid user interests.

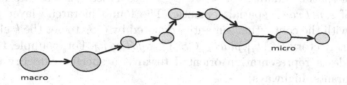

Fig. 2. Hybrid semantic trajectory.

The hybrid trajectory defines a trajectory associated with a hybrid space representation of different granularities according to the indoor and outdoor spaces, and where micro and macro places can be considered and a discrete representation of the spatial dimension (Fig. 2). For example, let us consider that the user interest denotes a high level of NO_2 exposition for a *place* spatial layer of interest and a *town* spatial layer of interest if user interests are not valid. In this case, the trajectory can be represented from a place (either in indoor or outdoor spaces) when the criteria are found and to a town when the criteria are not found and vice versa. In this example, all POIs belong to {*place, town*} layers.

Hybrid Trajectory Operations. In order to extract a hybrid representation of some semantic trajectories, let us introduce a series of basic operations that are embedded in Algorithm 1. Algorithm 1 shows the extraction process from a semantic trajectory to a hybrid trajectory.

Operation 1: is defined as:

$$f1: semTraj_{id} \times layer_1 \times layer_2 \to hybTraj_{id}$$

that takes as parameters a list of spatial layers of interests $layer_1 \in \mathbb{I}$ and $layer_2 \in \mathbb{O}$, or, $layer_1 \in \mathbb{O}$ and $layer_2 \in \mathbb{I}$. $f1$ extracts from the semantic trajectory the output hybrid semantic trajectory. The list of layers of interest represents the user's interest and refers to the indoor and outdoor spatial models. $\forall([t_i, t_j], Sem_k) \in semTraj_{id}$, $f1$ searches in the hierarchy of the spatial semantic the finest layer between $layer_1$ and $layer2$ denoted by $place_k$ and associate it with the contextual dimensions semantics denoted by CS_k to get the k element/segment of the hybrid trajectory $([t_i, t_j], place_k, CS_k) \in hybTraj_{id}$.

One may be interested in extracting a hybrid trajectory representation according to the semantic trajectory dimensions values. The following operation targets the spatial dimension category.

Operation 2: is defined as:

$$f2: semTraj_{id} \times layer_1 \times layer_2 \times SC \rightarrow hybTraj_{id}$$

where SC is set of geo-tagged semantic values related to *place* and $layer_1, layer_2 \in \mathbb{S}$ represent two layers of interest. $\forall([t_i, t_j], Sem_k) \in semTraj_{id}$, if $\exists sc \in SC$ where $sc \in place_k$ for $place_k \in Sem_k$, $f2$ searches for $layer_1$ hierarchy of spatial semantic of $semTraj_{id}$. Otherwise, $f2$ searches for $layer_2$ hierarchy of $semTraj_{id}$ spatial semantic. The found hierarchy layer $place_k$ is associated with the contextual semantics denoted by CS_k to get the k element of the hybrid trajectory $([t_i, t_j], place_k, CS_k) \in hybTraj_{id}$. For example, this operation provides a representation oriented towards a specific category of places (e.g., restaurants, highways).

The following operation focuses on the contextual dimension properties.

Operation 3: defined as:

$$f3: semTraj_{id} \times layer_1 \times layer_2 \times CV \rightarrow hybTraj_{id}$$

where CV is a set of contextual semantic values that belongs to C. $\forall([t_i, t_j], Sem_k) \in semTraj_{id}$, if $\exists cv \in CV$, where $cv \in Sem_k$, $f3$ searches for $layer_1$ hierarchy of $place_k$. Otherwise, $f3$ searches for $layer_2$ hierarchy of $place_k$. The resulting hierarchy layer $place_k$ is associated with the contextual dimensions semantics denoted by CS_k to get the k element of the hybrid trajectory $([t_i, t_j], place_k, CS_k) \in hybTraj_{id}$. For example, this operation provides a representation oriented towards specific contextual dimensions values (e.g., high pollution value, in a bus) to extract the hybrid spatial granule.

$layer_1$ and $layer_2$ represent two spatial layers. There are also optional parameters for all operations regarding the time interval and the contextual dimensions to consider in order to constrain the extraction scope if needed.

Algorithm 1. Extract hybrid trajectory with spatio-temporal aggregation

---

1: **input:** semantic trajectory $semTraj_{id}$; $UserInterests$: {$Spatial$:
$Layer, Contextual$: $Semantic$} where $Layer$ = {$layer_1 \in \mathbb{S}$, $layer_2 \in \mathbb{S}$ }
is a set of spatial layers of interest and $Semantic$ is a set of values of interest.
2: **output:** hybrid semantic trajectory $hybTraj_{id}$
3: $hybTraj_{id} \Leftarrow \emptyset$
4: **for each** $([t_i, t_j], Sem_k) \in semTraj_{id}$ **do**
5:     $place_k \Leftarrow \emptyset$
6:     $CS_k \Leftarrow \emptyset$
7:     $place_{k-1} \Leftarrow \emptyset$
8:     $CS_{k-1} \Leftarrow \emptyset$
9:     **if** $Semantic$ not null **then**
10:         **if** $Sem_k.findContextualInterests(Semantic)$ **then** ▷ //searches if one of
the contextual interests is valid
11:             $place_k \Leftarrow Sem_k.findSpatialLayer(layer_1)$
12:         **else**
13:             $CS_k \Leftarrow Sem_k.findSpatialLayer(layer_2)$ ▷ //returns a place at a
specific granularity
14:         **end if**
15:     **else**
16:         $place_k \Leftarrow Sem_k.findFinerLayer(layer_1, layer_2)$ ▷ //one indoor layer and
one outdoor layer
17:     **end if**
18:     $CS_k \Leftarrow Sem_k.getContextualDimensions()$
19:     $place_{k-1} \Leftarrow hybTraj_{id}.getPlace(k-1)$ ▷ //get the last $place$ in $hybTraj_{id}$
20:     $CS_{k-1} \Leftarrow hybTraj_{id}.getContextualDimensions(k-1)$ ▷ //get the last CS in
$hybTraj_{id}$
21:     **if** $place_{k-1} \neq \emptyset$ **AND** $place_{k-1} == place_k$ **AND** $CS_{k-1} == CS_k$ **then**
22:         $hybTraj_{id}.updateEndTimeInterval(k-1, t_j)$ ▷ //change end time
interval of segment k-1 with t_j
23:     **else**
24:         $hybTraj_{id}.addSegment([t_i, t_j], place_k, CS_k)$ ▷ //add a new segment
25:     **end if**
26: **end for**
27: **return** $hybTraj_{id}$

Contextual-based Trajectory Representation. The semantic trajectory
representation supports multiple dimensions, including the spatial and contextual ones. However, and in many cases, a user might require a specific view from
such a generic representation, and this by taking into account some contextual
criterion. For that purpose, we extend the generic model by the contextual-based semantic trajectory concept that aims to extract from the generic/flat
semantic trajectory representation a new one based on one context of interest.
A contextual-based semantic trajectory is denoted by:

$$contTraj_{id} = \{([t_{s1}, t_{e1}], coi_1, O_1), ([t_{s2}, t_{e2}], coi_2, O_2), ..., ([t_{sn}, t_{en}], coi_n, O_n)\}$$
$$(5)$$

coi_i represents the semantic value of the context of interest and it is denoted by $\{c : value\}$. O_i is a set of the other semantic values that holds during $[t_{si}, t_{ei}]$ where $t_{ei} < t_{si+1}$. In this case, O_i represents a set of semantic values, including the spatial semantic value except for the context of interest value.

For this representation, the user interest is considered as a unique contextual dimension/semantic of $c \in C$.

Algorithm 2. Extract contextual-based trajectory

1: **input:** semantic trajectory $semTraj_{id}$, a context of interest name $c \in C$
2: **output:** contextual-based semantic trajectory $contTraj_{id}$
3: $contTraj_{id} \Leftarrow \emptyset$
4: **for each** $([t_i, t_j], Sem_k) \in semTraj_{id}$ **do**
5:     $coi_k \Leftarrow \emptyset$
6:     $O_k \Leftarrow \emptyset$
7:     $coi_k \Leftarrow Sem_k.getContextualSemantic(c)$ $\triangleright$ //get the semantic value of the context of interests c
8:     $O_k \Leftarrow Sem_k.getOtherSemantics(c)$ $\triangleright$ //get all semantics, including spatial semantics, except for c. Spatial semantics include places with hierarchies
9:     $contTraj_{id}.addSegment([t_i, t_j], coi_k, O_k)$ $\triangleright$ //add a new segment
10: **end for**
11: **return** $contTraj_{id}$

Contextual-based Trajectory Operation. In order to extract the contextual-based representation of semantic trajectories, we introduced the following operator that is embedded in Algorithm 2. Algorithm 2 shows the extraction process from a semantic trajectory to a contextual-based trajectory. *Operation 4:* is defined as:

$$f4: semTraj_{id} \times c \rightarrow contTraj_{id}$$

that takes as parameter a contextual dimension name $c \in C$ and extract from the semantic trajectory the output contextual-based semantic trajectory. $\forall ([t_i, t_j], Sem_k) \in semTraj_{id}$, $f4$ searches for coi_k and O_k. This operation provides a representation that focuses on a specific contextual dimension to return an output of annotated time interval sequences of the specified context state associated with the remaining dimensions, including the spatial one.

5   Experimentation

Data Integration. This work has been experimented with real environmental crowd-sensing data collected in the region of Paris. Data have been obtained by the Polluscope project where participants were equipped with three sensors that record ambient air data (i.e., temperature, humidity, particulate matter:

$PM_{2.5}$, PM_{10}, $PM_{1.0}$, NO_2 and Black Carbon) and with a tablet embedding a GPS chipset that tracks their locations along their daily activities. Additionally, these trajectories have been manually self-annotated by the participants using their tablet to report on their activities and behaviours in both outdoor and indoor spaces. The activities last for a period of time and include transportation mode (e.g., car, bus, metro) as well as indoor (e.g., home, office, restaurant) and outdoor (e.g., park, street) activities. On the other side, behaviours are temporary acts for a short period of time and include actions related to air pollution (e.g., open a window, start cooking, smoking, turn on a chimney). The participants are anonymised. Our experiments have been implemented with a subset of trajectories over an average period of two weeks.

We used Vita generator [10] for synthetic trajectories in indoor environments since the collected data do not have precise localisation in indoor environments. We generated different indoor trajectories in one synthetic indoor building and where synthetic positioning devices (e.g., RFID) are also generated. Different moving object types were considered (e.g., destination, random-walk) as provided in Vita. A list of participants' trajectories working on the same site was selected then and merged with real outdoor trajectories according to the annotation "office" the participants indicated it using their toolkit. Data quality issues have not been considered so far, but this does not impact the principles behind our data integration and modelling approach.

Implementation. Figure 3 sketches an overview of the processing steps applied to generating semantic trajectories and their multiple views. Inputs of the framework are synchronised data flows for each participant. According to our spatial model, the synthetic spatial data of the indoor environment are merged with real spatial data of the outdoor environment. Spatial data are then characterised by external information and geo-tagged using OpenStreetMap (openstreetmap.org) (OSM) reverse geocoding. Time interval spatial sequences are extracted to form the spatial semantic sequences. On the other hand, contextual data are converted to time interval sequences, where time-series measures data are mapped to qualitative information.

Finally, all of these sequences are grouped in one sequence and segmented upon at least one dimension value change to get the multi-dimensional semantic trajectory sequences associated for each mobile user. Semantic trajectories produced are stored into a graph database. While the semantic trajectories could be stored using various relational database management systems, Neo4j has been logically selected since it is based on a graph-based data model and encompasses advanced data manipulation capabilities and computational efficiency [5]. Neo4j is an open-source Java-based graph database that allows extending its functionality with user-defined procedures. These procedures can be easily added as plugin packed in a .jar file so that they can be invoked directly from the Cypher query language. The two aforementioned algorithms, Algorithm 1 and Algorithm 2 have been implemented as user-defined procedures in Neo4j.

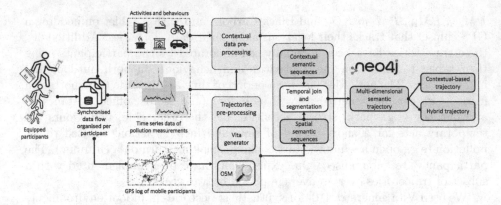

Fig. 3. Implementation methodology of our approach.

Experiments. For the sake of brevity, experiments are reported on the following three examples of operations:

(a) $f2$: $semTraj_{100} \times Road \times Town \times category$: $tourism \rightarrow hybTraj_{100}$
(b) $f3$: $semTraj_{100} \times Place \times County \times NO_2$: $High \rightarrow hybTraj_{100}$
(c) $f4$: $semTraj_{100} \times Activity \rightarrow contTraj_{100}$

The operation (a) extracts hybrid trajectories with 'Road' granularity when there is a *tourism* place, and 'Town' granularity otherwise. The operation (b) extracts hybrid trajectories with 'Place' granularity when there is a High level of NO_2 exposition, a 'County' granularity otherwise. The operation (c) extracts, from the semantic trajectories, contextual-based trajectories with the 'Activity' dimension.

In order to show differences between raw trajectories and different trajectory semantic representations, let us hereafter illustrate the output views of a portion of one trajectory in each representation and after each Neo4J graph operation. The experiments are applied on a participant trajectory of 40 min going from work office to home. The outputs can be explored interactively at the Neo4j interface level.

Let us apply operation (a) (query in Listing 1.1) to the same part of the trajectory to get the hybrid semantic trajectory illustrated in Fig. 4.

Listing 1.1. Query using operation (a) example

```
CALL multiViews.hybridTrajectoryGraph(100, {category:'tourism'}, 'Road',
    'County')
MATCH (poi:POI {participantID:'100'})
MATCH (poi)-[:HAS_NO2_SEMANTIC]->(no2:No2Semantic)
MATCH (poi)-[:HAS_PM10_SEMANTIC]->(pm10:Pm10Semantic)
MATCH (poi)-[:HAS_PM1_0_SEMANTIC]->(pm1:Pm1_0Semantic)
MATCH (poi)-[:HAS_PM2_5_SEMANTIC]->(pm2:Pm2_5Semantic)
MATCH (poi)-[:HAS_BC_SEMANTIC]->(bc:BCSemantic)
MATCH (poi)-[:HAS_TEMPERATURE_SEMANTIC]->(temp:TemperatureSemantic)
MATCH (poi)-[:HAS_HUMIDITY_SEMANTIC]->(hum:HumiditySemantic)
MATCH (poi)-[:HAS_ACTIVITY_SEMANTIC]->(act:ActivitySemantic)
```

```
MATCH (poi)-[:HAS_BEHAVIOUR_SEMANTIC]->(eve:BehaviourSemantic)
WHERE poi.start>='2019-11-30 15:36:00+01:00' AND poi.end<'2019-11-30
    16:16:00+01:00'
RETURN *
```

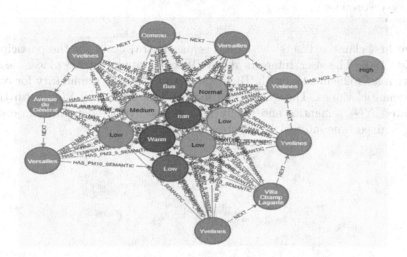

Fig. 4. Hybrid semantic trajectory path graph (operation (a)). Orange nodes represent *places* (at Road and County granularity) where time intervals are embedded. Coloured nodes represent other contextual dimensions.

The first clause calls the procedure that extracts the hybrid semantic trajectory for the participant with id '100'. The user interests are a 'Road' granularity for places with a 'tourism' category and a 'Town' granularity for others. The query then matches the extracted hybrid trajectory segments associated with multiple contextual semantics and returns a portion between a time interval. It returns the hybrid trajectory of the indicated time interval finally (illustrated in Fig. 4).

One can notice the semantic movement, represented by orange nodes, from 'Town' granularity to a finer place at the 'Road' granularity (Villa Champ Lagard) since the participant was in a place categorised by *tourism* in that road. Other nodes colours represent the different contextual semantics associated with the trajectory.

When applying the operation (b) (query in Listing 1.2) on the same portion, one get the hybrid semantic trajectory graph illustrated in Fig. 5.

Listing 1.2. Query using operation (b) example

```
CALL multiViews.hybridTrajectoryGraph(100, 'No2Semantic',{level:'High'},
    'Place', 'County')
MATCH (poi:POI {participantID:'100'})
MATCH (poi)-[:HAS_NO2_SEMANTIC]->(no2:No2Semantic)
WHERE poi.start>='2019-11-30 15:36:00+01:00' AND poi.end<'2019-11-30
    16:16:00+01:00'
RETURN *
```

The first clause extracts the hybrid semantic trajectory for the participant with id '100'. The user interests are a 'Place' granularity for places associated with a 'No2Semantic' with 'High' value and 'County' granularity for other 'No2Semantic' values. The query then matches the extracted POIs with their associated NO_2 semantics and finally returns the extracted hybrid trajectory during a given time interval (illustrated in Fig. 5).

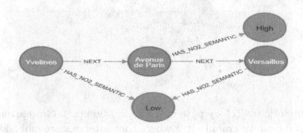

Fig. 5. Hybrid semantic trajectory path graph (operation (b)). Orange nodes represent *places* where time intervals are embedded. Blue nodes represent other contextual dimensions. We limit the contextual dimension to NO_2 semantic for clarification.

We hide all the dimensions except the NO_2 dimension for a better illustration. This highlights how spatial and temporal aggregations impact the trajectory to get a reduced view. This view shows the clear states of the trajectory regarding the user interests, high level of NO_2 at 'Road' granularity (Avenue de Paris) and 'Town' granularity for other NO_2 levels (Yvelines and Versailles).

Let us apply the operation (c) (query in Listing 1.3) on the same part of the trajectory to obtain the contextual-based trajectory on 'Activity' context of interest. The first clause extracts the contextual based semantic trajectory for the participant with id '100' and with 'ActivitySemantic' context of interest. Then, it matches the extracted *cois* and finally returns the contextual-based trajectory during an indicated time interval (illustrated in Fig. 6). Figure 6 shows a piece of this part so that we can clearly inspect the *cois* trajectory from 'Bus' to 'Rue' to 'Domicile'.

Listing 1.3. Query using operation (c) example

```
CALL multiViews.contextualBasedTrajectoryGraph(100 , 'ActivitySemantic')
MATCH (coi:COI {participantID:'100'})-[:HAS_PLACE]->(p:Place)
WHERE coi.start>='2019-11-30 15:36:00+01:00' AND coi.end<'2019-11-30
    16:16:00+01:00'
RETURN coi, p
```

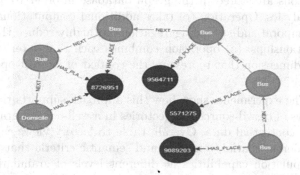

Fig. 6. Contextual-based semantic trajectory path graph (operation (c)). Orange nodes represent the context of interests (*coi*) where time intervals are embedded and brown nodes represent the spatial dimension (the spatial hierarchies are hidden for a better illustration).

Experimental Evaluation. The experimental evaluation has been performed on Neo4j 4.2.3 (Enterprise) running on Windows 10. The hardware configuration is as follows: 6 cores Intel(R) Core(TM) i7-8750H CPU @ 2.20 GHz, the machine has 32 GB in terms of RAM and a SSD storage of 239 GB.

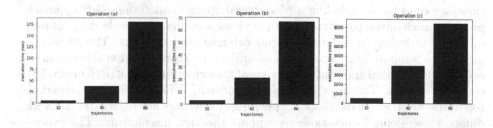

Fig. 7. Execution times of the operation examples

In order to evaluate the execution times of the different operations examples, three different databases have been prepared. The first one contains 10 semantic trajectories (98,530 nodes and 920,849 relationships), the second one 40 semantic trajectories (305,879 nodes and 2,838,387 relationships) and the third one

86 semantic trajectories (780,550 nodes and 7,393,761 relationships). Average execution times are presented in Fig. 7.

Execution times vary depending on the trajectories length and user interests. One can notice execution times relatively costly and that increase with the number of trajectories; this is due to the fact that these operations extract the entire trajectories and re-manage the representation for each trajectory according to the desired new representation that depends on the user interests. The results of these operations are stored in the graph database in order to apply further queries and analytics. Operation (c) takes additional computational time since there are no temporal and spatial aggregations to highly reduce the amount of nodes and relationships. (c) operation combines each time interval node with the contextual dimension that represents the context of interest operation.

Discussion. The experiments show how this approach supports the generation of different views of crowd-sourced trajectories in a well-defined graph structure with associated contextual data. Overall, these trajectory views can be derived according to different spatial, temporal and semantic criteria that provide flexible data manipulation capabilities at different levels of granularity and user interests. However, the intrinsic nature of such a model may involve some loss of information that may occur on some of the represented dimensions. The relevance of the whole data manipulation capabilities and performance figures still have to be experimented in a context of mobility patterns that arise in both outdoor and indoor spaces. As for now, outdoor trajectories only were derived from real data, although indoor trajectories were simulated. Last but not least, there is still a need to experiment with additional query mechanisms and data structures to improve computational times.

6   Conclusion

This paper develops a modelling approach for indoor and outdoor semantic trajectories in a crowd-sourcing environment where multiple dimensional annotations are considered, including a place-based spatial annotation. Our approach provides mechanisms to extract multiple views according to a wide range of user interests, including granularity, spatial category and contexts. The presented algorithms support from a continuous trajectory representation derivation of even a hybrid spatial and contextual view of trajectories from micro to macro levels and vice-versa. This approach has been formally defined and implemented on top of the Neo4j graph database. Cypher query language has been extended with different user-defined operations to support the view mechanisms. The experimentation illustrates the whole framework's potential, performance figures and its potential for trajectory data exploration, manipulation, and analysis. The work outcome is instrumental in supporting trajectory data analysis and exploring mobility patterns. As future works, we are developing a streaming system to apply the modelling approach to real-time detection of patterns over different levels of granularity. We are also planning to use the modelling approach for similarity measurement between trajectories.

References

1. Alvares, L.O., Bogorny, V., Kuijpers, B., de Macedo, J.A.F., Moelans, B., Vaisman, A.: A model for enriching trajectories with semantic geographical information. In: Proceedings of the 15th Annual ACM International Symposium on Advances in Geographic Information Systems, pp. 1–8 (2007)
2. Bogorny, V., Renso, C., de Aquino, A.R., de Lucca Siqueira, F., Alvares, L.O.: Constant-a conceptual data model for semantic trajectories of moving objects. Trans. GIS **18**(1), 66–88 (2014)
3. Cayèré, C., et al.: Multi-level and multiple aspect semantic trajectory model: application to the tourism domain. ISPRS Int. J. Geo-Inf. **10**(9), 592 (2021)
4. Fileto, R., May, C., Renso, C., Pelekis, N., Klein, D., Theodoridis, Y.: The baquara2 knowledge-based framework for semantic enrichment and analysis of movement data. Data Knowl. Eng. **98**, 104–122 (2015)
5. Gómez, L.I., Kuijpers, B., Vaisman, A.A.: Analytical queries on semantic trajectories using graph databases. Trans. GIS **23**(5), 1078–1101 (2019)
6. Ilarri, S., Stojanovic, D., Ray, C.: Semantic management of moving objects: a vision towards smart mobility. Exp. Syst. Appl. **42**(3), 1418–1435 (2015)
7. Izquierdo, Y.T., et al.: Stop-and-move sequence expressions over semantic trajectories. Int. J. Geog. Inf. Sci. **35**(4), 793–818 (2021)
8. Jin, M., Claramunt, C.: A semantic model for human mobility in an urban region. J. Data Seman. **7**(3), 171–187 (2018)
9. Kontarinis, A., Zeitouni, K., Marinica, C., Vodislav, D., Kotzinos, D.: Towards a semantic indoor trajectory model: application to museum visits. GeoInformatica **25**(2), 311–352 (2021). https://doi.org/10.1007/s10707-020-00430-x
10. Li, H., Lu, H., Chen, X., Chen, G., Chen, K., Shou, L.: Vita: a versatile toolkit for generating indoor mobility data for real-world buildings. Proc. VLDB Endowment **9**(13), 1453–1456 (2016)
11. Mello, R.D.S., et al.: Master: a multiple aspect view on trajectories. Trans. GIS **23**(4), 805–822 (2019)
12. Noureddine, H., Ray, C., Claramunt, C.: Semantic trajectory modelling in indoor and outdoor spaces. In: 2020 21st IEEE International Conference on Mobile Data Management (MDM), pp. 131–136. IEEE (2020)
13. Noureddine, H., Ray, C., Claramunt, C.: A hierarchical indoor and outdoor model for semantic trajectories. Trans. GIS **26**(1), 214–235 (2022). https://doi.org/10.1111/tgis.12841
14. Noureddine, H., Ray, C., Claramunt, C.: Multiple views of semantic trajectories in indoor and outdoor spaces. In: Proceedings of the 29th International Conference on Advances in Geographic Information Systems (2021)
15. Parent, C., et al.: Semantic trajectories modeling and analysis. ACM Comput. Surv. (CSUR) **45**(4), 1–32 (2013)
16. Pelekis, N., Theodoridis, Y., Janssens, D.: On the management and analysis of our lifesteps. ACM SIGKDD Explor. Newsl. **15**(1), 23–32 (2014)
17. Spaccapietra, S., Parent, C., Damiani, M.L., de Macedo, J.A., Porto, F., Vangenot, C.: A conceptual view on trajectories. Data Knowl. Eng. **65**(1), 126–146 (2008)
18. Zheni, D., Frihida, A., Claramunt, C., Ben Ghezala, H.: A semantic-based data model for the manipulation of trajectories: application to urban transportation. In: Gensel, J., Tomko, M. (eds.) W2GIS 2015. LNCS, vol. 9080, pp. 124–142. Springer, Cham (2015). https://doi.org/10.1007/978-3-319-18251-3_8

Impact of COVID-19 on Tourists' Travel Intentions and Behaviors: The Case Study of Hong Kong, China

Yang Xu[1,2], Peng Peng[1(✉)], Christophe Claramunt[1,3], and Feng Lu[1,2]

[1] State Key Laboratory of Resources and Environmental Information System, Institute of Geographic Sciences and Natural Resources Research, Chinese Academy of Sciences, Beijing 100864, China
pengp@lreis.ac.cn
[2] College of Resources and Environment, University of Chinese Academy of Sciences, Beijing 100864, China
[3] Naval Academy Research Institute, 29240 Lanvéoc, France

Abstract. Over the past two years, the COVID-19 pandemic had a major worldwide health, economic and daily life impact. Amongst many dramatic consequences, such as major human mobility disruptions at all scales, the tourism sector has been largely affected. This raises the need for the development of quantitative and qualitative research to favor a better understanding of the impact of the pandemic on human travel behaviors. This study introduces a computational approach that combines inference mechanisms and statistics to quantify tourists' travel behaviors before and during the pandemic by exploring the evolution of the patterns extracted from a local tourism social network from 2019 to 2020 in the city of Hong Kong. The results show that the COVID-19 pandemic: 1) has a major influence on travel intentions that mainly swift from journeys with generally long sequences of attractions to rather single attractions; 2) lead to a decline when considering connections between popular attractions, while the strength of connections within other attractions increase; 3) generates novel patterns such as tourists preferring relaxing visits and even minor attractions.

Keywords: COVID-19 · Travel intention and behavior · Social media data · Tourism network

1 Introduction

Tourism is nowadays one of the worldwide fastest growing and most dynamic emerging industry and a major player of the world economy development. Many cities strongly rely on their tourism industry for the development of their economy. However, the tourism industry has experienced an unprecedented loss due to the COVID-19 pandemic that started in December 2019. The United Nations World Tourism Organization (UNWTO) estimates that international tourism sector has been 20–30% lower in 2020 than in 2019.

© Springer Nature Switzerland AG 2022
F. Karimipour and S. Storandt (Eds.): W2GIS 2022, LNCS 13238, pp. 18–27, 2022.
https://doi.org/10.1007/978-3-031-06245-2_2

Since the COVID-19 outbreak, activities that involve a high level of human interactions, like tourism, cannot continue as they have done in the past [1].

During this COVID-19 outbreak, many tourists regard popular and gathering attractions as high-risk destinations. Previous studies reveal that tourists' post-disaster travel behaviors can be influenced by their risk perceptions [2, 3] and motivations [4, 5]. The impact of COVID-19 is not only dramatic on tourists' travel behavior, but also on the way tourists behave, perceive the environment and act while travelling. For example, a study shows how the current health crisis affects travelers' preferences between crowded and non-crowded options [6]. It has been observed that threat severity and susceptibility can cause 'travel fear', which leads to protection motivation and protective travel intentions during and even after the pandemic outbreak [7]. A methodology has been suggested to measure the intra-personal anxiety of travelers (and non- travelers) and pandemic-induced changes in tourist beliefs and travel behaviors [8]. Quantitatively grasping the changing characteristics of people's travel intention and behavior before and after the pandemic is of great significance to the reshaping of the tourism market after the epidemic. Pandemic also decreases tourists' time and frequency to travel outside, with limited tourism connections and collaboration. For example, tourism in Kashmir had a fast decrease and local economic groups were deeply affected due to the COVID-19 lockdown [9]. Although there is a boom in studies addressing the impact of COVID-19 on tourism activities [10], seldom researches have qualitatively examined tourists' intentions and behaviour. To bridge this gap, our study aims to conduct a comparative quantitative analysis before and during the pandemic to have a global view of the COVID-19 impact.

With the development of the digital era and social networks, tourists' footprints and check-in data are nowadays widely available, this opening many opportunities for extracting travel flows within and between different tourism attractions, and even analyzing such patterns at the city or country levels using network-based models and approaches [11–13]. A quantitative method has been introduced for investigating the network characteristics of drive tourism destinations with the help of methodologies derived from network analysis [14]. Network analysis measures can classify destinations considering the routes of a self-organized tourists' samples that visited more than one destination in Sicily [15]. The characteristics associated with the spatial network structure of the tourism economy has been examined by adopting the tourism economic gravity model and social network analysis [16]. Overall, these studies give us a sound theoretical background for studying the impact of the COVID-19 on the tourism network.

Hong Kong is well-known as a shopping paradise. Every year, a large number of tourists worldwide come to Hong Kong to travel and go shopping. We select it as a case study area and propose an approach based on statistics and network theory. The approach is based on an extraction of tourists' footprints from the TripAdvisor website which has abundant travel records worldwide and provides a valuable resource to evaluate the impact of COVID-19 on the Hong Kong tourism industry from 2019 to 2020, so before and during the pandemic. To this end, we propose an approach based on statistics to quantify tourists' travel intention, then we conduct a tourism network analysis to detect change of tourists' behaviors. Last a series of geo-visualization of the structuration of the tourism network provides a support for an intuitive perception of the impact of the pandemic on tourism activities in an urban environment.

2   Materials and Methodology

2.1   Data Collection

The main data source is extracted from qualitative comments made from a well-known tourism website TripAdvisor (https://www.tripadvisor.com/) that generates user's footprints during 2019.1–2020.12. The principles applied for the generation of a footprint database are illustrated (see Fig. 1). Firstly, all attractions in Hong Kong are crawled from a TripAdvisor attraction list. Next, a webpage cleaning is applied to get both comment times and travel times from the reviews page of each attraction (i.e., to avoid differences between comment times and real travel times). Finally, digital footprints are generated by sorting all visitor's travel times and users' itinerary.

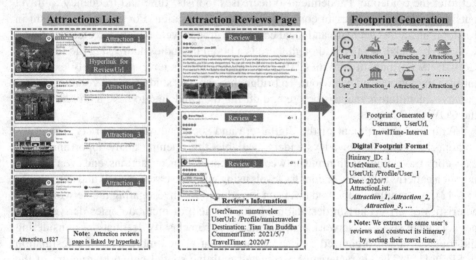

Fig. 1.   Footprint generation processing.

2.2   Methodology

Figure 2 shows the main principles behind our approach. The study first extracts tourists' comments from the TripAdvisor website and generates tourists' footprints by sorting their travel times. TripAdvisor website covers tourists' comments on worldwide attractions, with an average monthly visit of 415 million times. The tourism network extracted from tourists' footprints is based on attraction's co-occurrence. Finally, a statistical analysis is conducted to evaluate tourists' travel behaviors. We apply a series of network indices such as weighted degree and strength to explore the evolution of the Hong Kong tourism network from 2019 to 2020. The objective is to analyze changes of tourists' intentions and behaviors via semantic and spatio-temporal analysis applied to the evolution of the Hong Kong tourism network.

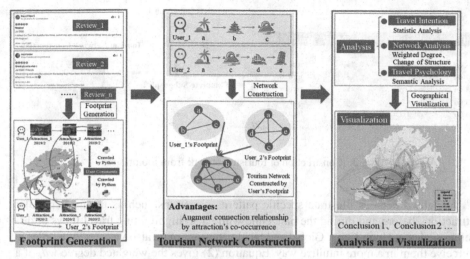

Fig. 2. Conceptual processing graph.

Tourists' Behavior Assessment. Our study introduces an approach based on statistical analysis to quantify tourists' travel intentions and behaviors. In order to take into account tourists' behaviors according to different waves of COVID-19 [17], tourists' footprints are sorted by month to aggregate them at a comprehensive level of temporal granularity. We introduced an index named Intention-Index-Value (I-I-V) to evaluate tourists' travel intention, Eq. (1) gives the definition of I-I-V. $Volume_{(total)}$ denotes the total number of footprint records in one month, $Volume_{(i)}$ denotes the amounts of footprints which contain i attractions in one month. High I-I-V values denote situations in which tourists prefer itineraries with rather single attractions, while low I-I-V values are likely to show cases where tourists prefer itineraries with rather long sequences of attractions.

$$\text{I-I-V} = Normalize \left(\sum_{i=1}^{N} \frac{Volume_{(total)}}{Volume_{(i)}} \times i \right) \tag{1}$$

Tourism Network Construction and Analysis. The attraction network of Hong Kong is based on the co-occurrence of different attractions in tourists' footprints, and where each footprint is transferred into a complete subgraph of the entire attraction network (see Fig. 3). The weight of a given edge between two attraction nodes denotes their co-occurrence frequency derived from all footprints. Moreover, every pair of connected attractions are associated to one itinerary, so each tourist's digital footprint generates a complete subgraph whose nodes are attractions and connections denote attractions parts of one of her/his itinerary (Fig. 3 left). Finally, the whole subgraphs are combined into an entire tourism network (Fig. 3 right).

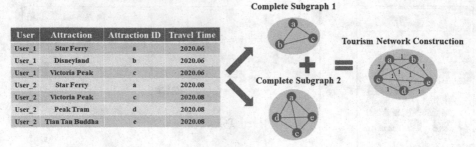

Fig. 3. Construction of tourism network from footprints.

Weighted degrees illustrate specific patterns variations such as the most popular attractions before and during the pandemic while also highlighting travel flows at different scales in Hong Kong. Global and local patterns can be also visualized in order to perceive them in a more intuitive way. Equation (2) gives the weighted degree wd_i of a node i, where i denotes a given attraction, j all other attractions and E_{ij} is valued by the unit when two attractions appear in a given itinerary and null otherwise.

$$wd_i = \sum_j E_{ij} \qquad (2)$$

Therefore, changes of tourists' behavior are detected via semantic analysis conducted with statistical and evolution analysis of the local tourism network. Based on the *top@10* negative growth rate in 2020 and popular attractions in 2019 and 2020, patterns of change are analyzed and illustrated using a word cloud technique to show the evolution of tourists' behaviors.

3 Experimental Results

3.1 Assessing Tourists' Travel Intentions

Figure 4 left shows the main tourism patterns of each month from 2019.1 to 2020.12 and the successive decline of tourists' flows. In 2019, the peak tourist season is concentrated in January, March, April and October probably due to the opening of students in March and April, and the National Day holiday in October. With then a continuous decline probably due to an influence of local protests in Hong Kong, there is also a local phenomenon in March, April and October with slight recovery of tourists' numbers than other month in 2019 with a slight growth rate. Due to local lockdown and travel restrictions from 18 January 2020 to 22 April 2020, it clearly appears that the amounts of tourists dramatically felt in 2020 to then reach very low numbers from March to the end of the year (see Fig. 4 right). This shows that the tourism sector has been affected really hard by the COVID-19 pandemic.

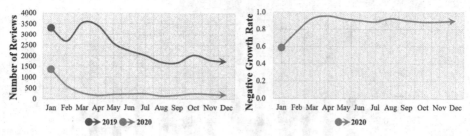

Fig. 4. Tourists number and negative growth rate in Hong Kong during 2019–2020.

In order to get into more details regarding the practical impact of these falling patterns, we generated tourists' digital footprints by sorting their travel times and counting the number of attractions in each travel footprint (Fig. 5). It appears that 1057 footprints with one attraction were recorded in 2019, but only 567 in the same period in 2020, and in other month, the difference became bigger. Similarly, 753 footprints have more than five attractions in 2019, but only 75 footprints have more than five attractions in 2019. I-I-V result is derived and shown in Fig. 6. It appears that although footprints with one attraction had a sharp decline in 2020, still this type of footprint always has a leading position. One can remark that footprints with more than one attraction are popular in 2019 but almost not in 2020. One can also infer from this result that the COVID-19 pandemic not only affects the number of attractions a tourist visits, but also impact multi-attractions travel when tourists visit many attractions in one trip. The results also showed that tourists are nowadays very likely to minimize interactions while travelling due to health protection constraints and motivation.

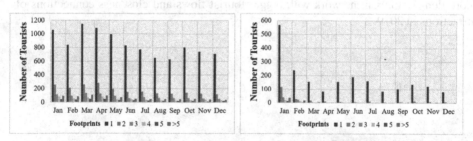

Fig. 5. Tourists numbers distribution of different footprints to Hong Kong in 2019 (left) and 2020 (right). (Note that the Footprints represent number of attractions in each travel itinerary)

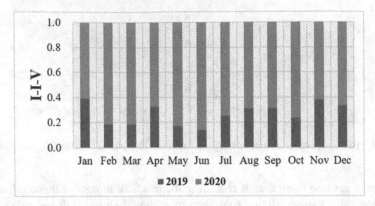

Fig. 6. I-I-V result in 2019 and 2020.

3.2 Tourism Network Changes

For a better understanding of the impact of the COVID-19 on the tourists' behavior, a tourism network analysis has been conducted together with a geo-visualization of the Hong Kong tourism network as shown in Fig. 6. It appears that not only the structure of the whole tourism network has changed, but also the top 10 popular attractions. As shown in Fig. 7 left, the leftmost attraction is Hong Kong-Zhuhai-Macao Bridge in 2019. This attraction not only has many cooperation with local attractions in Hong Kong, but also acted as an intermediary and a bridge between Hong Kong and Chinese mainland. In 2020 (see Fig. 7 right), the network structure of tourism was loose, with limited important tourism connections and collaboration. These results showed that there is a more density tourism network with bigger tourist flows and closeness connections of attractions in 2019.

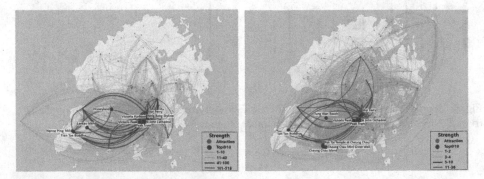

Fig. 7. Tourism network based on footprints of Hong Kong in 2019 (left) and 2020 (right).

The average degree and network density were derived for assessing the whole network, as well as the local degrees and weighted degrees to have a micro perspective. Generally, high average degree and density denote that network has more efficiency and connections respectively, and we inferred that the Hong Kong tourism network has a higher cooperation efficiency in 2019 than 2020 as the average degree in 2019 (88.67) is higher than 2020 (52.04). Similarly, network density in 2019 (0.138) is higher than 2020 (0.101). These results all can explain that tourism network in 2019 has closer connection and cooperation, while being more density and robust than in 2020. Additional indices were applied to evaluate the vital attractions in the tourism network. Table 1 shows the top 10 weighted degrees that reflect the importance of attractions. It appears that Victoria Peak, Star Ferry, Tian tan Buddha, Peak Tram, St john Cathedral are all amongst the top 10 attractions in 2019 and 2020. However, the most popular attractions like Ngong Ping 360, Hong Kong Disneyland don't show up in 2020 probably due to these are all overcrowded places, as well as tourists visiting these places are usually not locals. In contrast, some previously minor attractions like Tung Wan Beach, Cheung Chau Rock Cravings and so on have broken into top 10 popular attractions in 2020. These attractions have some common features: they are all minor and relaxing places. In order to explicitly detect the change of tourists' behavior, we analyze the change of theme based on popular attractions in 2019 and 2020, and apply a word cloud technique to show the evolution of tourists' behaviors (see Fig. 8). This result illustrates that after lockdown measures announced, threat severity and susceptibility can cause protection motivation and protective travel behaviors after the pandemic outbreak, tourists may choose minor and relaxing place to release their pressure. We also find that the spatial distribution of top 10 attractions reveals an important difference when comparing 2019 and 2020 figures (Fig. 7.)

Table 1. Node index characteristics.

Rank	2019		2020	
	Attraction	Weighted degree	Attraction	Weighted degree
1	Victoria Peak	4030	Star Ferry	386
2	Star Ferry	4013	Victoria Peak	325
3	Tian Tan Buddha	2380	St John Cathedral	260
4	Hong Kong Skyline	2009	Tian Tan Buddha	233
5	Ngong Ping 360	1610	Peak Tram	213
6	Disneyland	1366	Cheung Chau Mini Great Wall	201
7	Peak Tram	1108	Cheung Chau Island	198
8	Victoria Harbor	859	Pak Tai Temple	197
9	St John Cathedral	785	Tung Wan Beach	192
10	Lantau island	781	Cheung Chau Rock Carvings	192

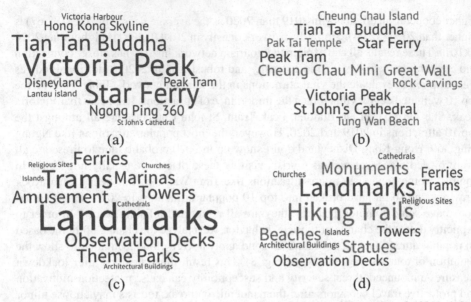

Fig. 8. Change of popular attractions and related semantic theme of Hong Kong in 2019 (left) and 2020 (right).

4   Conclusion

The outbreak of the COVID-19 pandemic had a devastating impact on our daily life and brought the tourism industry to a major breakdown. Figuring out the impact of COVID-19 on the tourism network is still an area that deserves additional quantitative studies to provide a better understanding of the real novel patterns that emerge. This research introduces a quantitative and statistical analysis of the evolution of the Hong Kong tourism network before and during the COVID-19 pandemic. We apply a network analysis to study the tourism network of Hong Kong in 2019 and 2020 using tourists' footprints extracted from the TripAdvisor website. The results show that: 1) the pandemic have huge impact on tourists' travel behavior, the specific performance is tourists' travel intentions have changed from itineraries with long sequence of attractions to itineraries with single attraction. 2) COVID-19 led to a decline in the strength of connections between popular attractions, but the strength of connections within minority attractions continues to increase. 3) tourists' behaviors have been changed, relaxing and minority attractions in the past are more fascinating at present. For instance, the top 10 popular attractions in 2020 were different from 2019. People always choose the most popular attraction to travel before the pandemic, like Victoria Peak, Disneyland, etc. But they may choose a more relaxing and minority attraction to travel like Tung Wan Beach, Cheung Chau Rock Cravings during the pandemic.

Finally, this work can be extended towards several directions. First, using a similar methodology, tourism patterns before and during the pandemic can be applied to different cities to cross-analysis the impact of different lock-down measures. Furthermore, the possible recovery of the tourism industry might be nowadays studied as the number of lock-down measures is likely to be relaxed, but maybe not the way tourist might behave in the changing world and by also considering the increasing impact of environment protection policies.

References

1. Wen, J., Kozak, M., Yang, S., et al.: COVID-19: potential effects on Chinese citizens' lifestyle and travel. Tourism Rev. (2020)
2. Chew, E.Y.T., Jahari, S.A.: Destination image as a mediator between perceived risks and revisit intention: a case of post-disaster Japan. Tour. Manage. **40**, 382–393 (2014)
3. Su, Y., Zhao, F., Tan, L.: Whether a large disaster could change public concern and risk perception: a case study of the 7/21 extraordinary rainstorm disaster in Beijing in 2012. Nat. Hazards **78**(1), 555–567 (2015)
4. Biran, A., Liu, W., Li, G., Eichhorn, V.: Consuming post-disaster destinations: the case of Sichuan. China. Ann. Tourism Res. **47**, 1–17 (2014)
5. Rittichainuwat, N.: Responding to disaster: Thai and Scandinavian tourists' motivation to visit phuket. Thailand. J. Travel Res. **46**(4), 422–432 (2008)
6. In-Jo, P., et al.: Impact of the COVID-19 pandemic on travelers' preference for crowded versus non-crowded options. Tourism Manag. (2021)
7. Dza, B., Qlc, D., Bwr, B.: Afraid to travel after COVID-19? Self-protection, coping and resilience against pandemic 'travel fear'. Tourism Manag. **83** (2020)
8. Zenker, S., Braun, E., Gyimóthy, S.: Too afraid to Travel? Development of a pandemic (COVID-19) anxiety travel scale (PATS). Tour. Manage. **84**(5), 104286 (2021)
9. Singh, A.L., Jamal, S., Ahmad, W.S.: Impact assessment of Lockdown amid covid-19 pandemic on tourism industry of Kashmir Valley, India. Res. Globalization, 100053 (2021)
10. Zenker, S., Kock, F.: The coronavirus pandemic – a critical discussion of a tourism research agenda. Tour. Manage. **81**(4), 104164 (2020)
11. Del Mondo, G., Peng, P., Gensel, J., et al.: Leveraging spatio-temporal graphs and knowledge graphs: perspectives in the field of maritime transportation. ISPRS Int. J. Geo Inf. **10**(8), 541 (2021)
12. Peng, P., et al.: A fine-grained perspective on the robustness of global cargo ship transportation networks. J. Geog. Sci. **28**(7), 881–889 (2018). https://doi.org/10.1007/s11442-018-1511-z
13. Peng, P., Yang, Y., Cheng, S.F., et al.: Hub-and-spoke structure: characterizing the global crude oil transport network with mass vessel trajectories. Energy **168**, 966–974 (2019)
14. Shih, H.Y.: Network characteristics of drive tourism destinations: an application of network analysis in tourism. Tour. Manage. **27**(5), 1029–1039 (2006)
15. D'Agata, R., Tomaselli, V.: Classifying tourism destinations: an application of network analysis. In: Giudici, P., Ingrassia, S., Vichi, M. (eds.) Statistical Models for Data Analysis. Studies in Classification, Data Analysis, and Knowledge Organization. Springer, Heidelberg (2013). https://doi.org/10.1007/978-3-319-00032-9_12
16. Gan, C., Voda, M., Wang, K., et al.: Spatial network structure of the tourism economy in urban agglomeration: a social network analysis. J. Hosp. Tour. Manag. **47**(6), 124–133 (2021)
17. Kan, Z., Kwan, M P., Huang, J., et al.: Comparing the space-time patterns of high-risk areas in different waves of COVID-19 in Hong Kong. Trans. GIS (2021)

Post-analysis of OSM-GAN Spatial Change Detection

Lasith Niroshan[(⊠)] and James D. Carswell

Technological University Dublin, Dublin, Ireland
D19126805@mytudublin.ie, james.carswell@TUDublin.ie

Abstract. Keeping crowdsourced maps up-to-date is important for a wide range of location-based applications (route planning, urban planning, navigation, tourism, etc.). We propose a novel map updating mechanism that combines the latest freely available remote sensing data with the current state of online vector map data to train a Deep Learning (DL) neural network. It uses a Generative Adversarial Network (GAN) to perform image-to-image translation, followed by segmentation and raster-vector comparison processes to identify changes to map features (e.g. buildings, roads, etc.) when compared to existing map data. This paper evaluates various GAN models trained with sixteen different datasets designed for use by our change detection/map updating procedure. Each GAN model is evaluated quantitatively and qualitatively to select the most accurate DL model for use in future spatial change detection applications.

Keywords: Generative Adversarial Networks · OpenStreetMap · Remote sensing · Spatial change detection

1 Introduction

Conventional (manual) crowdsourced map updating procedures utilises remote sensing imagery as a background layer to guide mappers as they manually digitise objects (e.g. buildings, roads, etc.). For example, OpenStreetMap (OSM) allows for the use of multiple satellite image sources when updating their maps [1]. However, to detect changes in satellite imagery *automatically* when comparing to the latest versions of online vector maps is an important next step for many GIScience related problems, including mapping.

Previously, we introduced our methodology for detecting changes (both constructions and destructions) between vector maps and raster images [2]. Consequently, a series of experiments was conducted to evaluate the accuracy of this OSM-GAN procedure. This paper reports on these experiments and other related outcomes of OSM-GAN predictions with various datasets.

Specifically, this study evaluates the prediction accuracy of various OSM-GAN models on several spatial datasets to select the best change detection model for use in further map updating operations. Two different raster and vector data sources were tested: 8-bit (panchromatic) and 24-bit (RGB) raster image data with spatial resolution 15 cm/pixel and 30 cm/pixel [5] and; OpenStreetMap (OSM) vector map data plus Ordnance Survey

© Springer Nature Switzerland AG 2022
F. Karimipour and S. Storandt (Eds.): W2GIS 2022, LNCS 13238, pp. 28–42, 2022.
https://doi.org/10.1007/978-3-031-06245-2_3

Ireland[1] (OSi) building footprint data of Dublin city centre were also used in conjunction with the raster data mentioned above.

1.1 Data Sources

Raster Data

Raster satellite image data was used to train the OSM-GAN models for detecting any changes to the map in a given Area of Interest (AoI). First, a satellite image dataset was created using freely available Google Earth satellite images discovered online using customised data *crawlers* that considers both spatial resolution (15 cm and 30 cm) and AoI. Second, a 25 cm resolution aerial orthophoto dataset of Dublin area registered to the Irish Transverse Mercator (ITM) coordinate system was acquired from OSi with an academic research license.

These TIFF (Tagged Image File Format) orthophotos needed to be pre-processed before inputting to the deep neural network – e.g., resampled to 30 cm pixels, co-registered, tiled, and served from QGIS[2]. Figure 1 shows the qualitative differences between both data sources (Google Earth and OSi). Note how some buildings currently visible in the Google Earth imagery are not present in the OSi orthophotos as they have since been demolished in preparation for constructing the new TU Dublin campus.

Fig. 1. Comparison of Google Earth satellite images (first row) and OSi aerial ortho images (second row) of the same AoI around Grangegorman, Dublin. The displayed resolution for both is 30 cm/pixel. The Google Earth images appear more vivid, the OSi images can be obtained at a higher resolution.

Vector Data

OSM vector data was the primary map data source checked for changes in this study. As OSi building footprint (vector) data is produced by Ireland's National Mapping Agency, it was used as ground truth for model training and prediction purposes. The OSM vector

---

[1] https://osi.ie/.

[2] https://docs.qgis.org/3.16/en/docs/user_manual/preamble/preamble.html.

data was downloaded using their *Overpass* API [3] by first parsing the minimum bounding rectangle (MBR) of a user generated AoI. The OSi building footprints were provided in DWG (AutoCAD) format. A series of operations converted the DWG formatted data into *GeoJSON* format to be compatible with further processing steps. Table 1 gives a summary of both the OSM and OSi building footprint datasets.

Table 1. Details of the two vector datasets.

	OSM dataset	OSi dataset
Area of interests	Selective areas around Grangegorman, Dublin	*53.3514000, −6.2892000, 53.3596000, −6.2730000*
Number of objects	15,000+	3036
Spatial reference system	EPSG:3857 (Spherical Mercator projection)	Irish Transverse Mercator (ITM)
License	Open Database License (ODbL)	OSi License
Data format	JSON, GeoJSON	DWG

1.2 The *Kay* Supercomputer

The Irish Centre for High-End Computing (ICHEC) allows institutional users (e.g. academic researchers) access to its super computing infrastructure, named *Kay* [4]. Kay is comprised of five sub-components: Cluster, GPU, Phi, High Memory, and Service and Storage. Specifically, for experiments in this study, the GPU service was utilised.

The GPU service is a partition of 16 nodes where each node has 2×20-core 2.4 GHz Intel Xeon Gold 6148 (Skylake) processors, 192 GiB of RAM, a 400 GiB local SSD for scratch space and a 100 Gbit Omni-Path network adaptor. Two NVIDIA Tesla V100 16 GB PCIe (Volta architecture) GPUs are integrated on each node. Each GPU has 5,120 CUDA cores and 640 Tensor Cores. In order to reduce training times, this study tested the Kay Supercomputer with various parameter settings [4]. As such, overall training times per model reduced from a few days spent training on a high-end "gamer spec" laptop, to just a few hours on Kay.

2 Related Work

Spatial change detection is a well-researched area in both the GIScience and computer vision domains. Historically, many different image processing techniques, including Markov Random Field [6] and Principal Component Analysis [7], were used to perform spatial change detection operations. More recently, artificial neural network-based techniques have been introduced to address various limitations of more traditional approaches (e.g. to overcome low performance, low segmentation accuracy, higher time complexity, etc.).

Now, common solutions to this problem rely on applying Machine Learning (ML) techniques such as *U-Net* [8], *SegNet* [9, 10], *Mask R-CNN* [11], and *Pix2Pix* among others [12, 13]. These approaches follow the encoder-decoder architecture to perform *image segmentation*, a critical step in any change detection process. In particular to GIS, image segmentation attempts to isolate various entities in the environment visible in aerial imagery. For example, entities such as buildings [14–16], road networks [17–24], and land-use classifications [25–28].

With the emergence of Generative Adversarial Networks (GANs), image segmentation procedures have been redefined as image-to-image *translation*. GANs are a ML technique of training a generative neural network model by representing the task as a supervised learning problem with two sub-models: a *generator* that learns to generate new examples; and a *discriminator* that tries to classify these generated examples as either *real* or *fake* (generated) [29]. Several studies have proposed GAN-based solutions for various spatial change detection problems, such as generating heat-maps of possible changes [30], seasonal change detection [31], and image classifications [32].

2.1 OSM-GAN for Spatial Change Detection

The OSM-GAN approach presented in this paper suggests a change detection methodology that employs spatial imagery (satellite images) and OSM vector map data [2] to train its models. The deep learning model should be accurate enough to detect image objects (e.g. buildings) to predict any change detection outcomes to these map features. Technically, the OSM-GAN model needs to perform a satellite image to feature-map translation with a high confidence level [2]. This paper proposes a methodology to evaluate various GAN models (trained with different datasets to perform satellite image to feature-map translation) to detect spatial changes accurately.

Producing our OSM-GAN model begins with the data *crawling* process. Freely available raster and vector data sources are crawled (mined) and saved in local directory structures ready for further processing. Geo-referenced satellite images are merged to construct the left half of the training sample, and OSM vectors are merged into a binary (black & white) single image to create the right half of the training sample. This process results in a single 600 × 300 pixel sized training sample as shown in Fig. 2.

Fig. 2. One sample of the OSM-GAN training dataset. The left side illustrates the satellite image component, and the right side shows the corresponding *feature-map*.

An object-density based data filtering mechanism is used to remove false-negative data samples from the training dataset [2]. The filtered dataset is then split into a 3:2 ratio of *training:validation* sets of data. Finally, these datasets were fed into the training algorithm on the Kay supercomputer to generate the resulting OSM-GAN model.

To initiate the change detection process, a *feature-map* (binary image that represents particular map features (e.g. buildings) as white blobs) needs to be predicted for a particular satellite image using the OSM-GAN model generated previously. Then the predicted feature-map is segmented into separate objects and compared to current OSM vector data using an Overlap Score Matrix (percent overlap of a feature-map object and its OSM vector footprint). Finally, any detected changes are post-processed to compose OSM-acceptable *changesets*. Figure 3 illustrates the overall workflow for spatial change detection based on OSM-GAN.

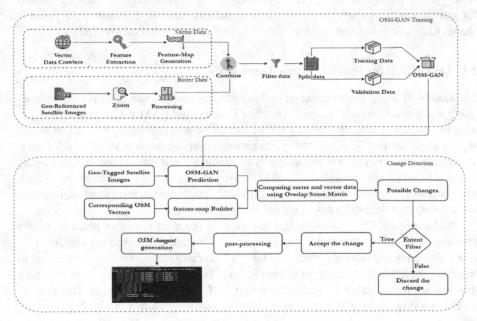

Fig. 3. System architecture of proposed OSM-GAN methodology for spatial change detection.

3   Experiments and Results

For this study, a series of experiments were conducted to evaluate the accuracy of OSM-GAN models qualitatively and quantitatively. Sixteen OSM-GAN models were trained with different datasets. A combination of two different spatial resolutions (15 cm and 30 cm) with two different types of images (panchromatic and RGB) were used to create the raster image segment (left half of the training sample). OSM and OSi vector data were used to create the right half of the training sample (Fig. 2). For instance, the

Google_OSi_8bit_z19 dataset was created from panchromatic (8-bit) Google Earth satellite images with 30 cm/pixel and OSi vectors. After the training process, the final model is named the same as the name of the dataset used to create it.

3.1 Modelling OSM-GAN with OSi Data

OSi raster (orthophotos resampled to 30 cm and 15 cm pixels to match the satellite data) and vector building footprint data was used in this experiment. Four datasets with different spatial resolutions and bit-depth were created from the above-mentioned sources. These datasets were smaller than the OSM datasets since the data provided by OSi was of a limited area of Dublin city centre only. Table 2 summarises the two datasets produced for this experiment.

Table 2. Details of datasets used in OSi-OSi experiment

	Dataset 1	Dataset 2	Dataset 3	Dataset 4
Raster source	OSi Orthophotos			
Vector source	OSi building footprints			
Resolution	30 cm (*z19*)		15 cm (*z20*)	
Bit-depth	8-bit	24-bit	8-bit	24-bit
Number of samples	581	581	1949	1949
Model ID	OP_OSi_8bit_z19	OP_OSi_24bit_z19	OP_OSi_8bit_z20	OP_OSi_24bit_z20

Upon completion of the training process, each model was evaluated on a new dataset within the same AoI. These results were qualitatively and quantitatively evaluated, and Accuracy, Recall, Precision and F1 score measurements were calculated for each model (Table 3). The model trained with 30 cm/pixel resolution RGB images can be considered more accurate than the other three models.

Table 3. Quantitative evaluation of the model trained with OSi Orthophoto and OSi vector data

Model ID	Accuracy	Precision	Recall	F1 score
OP_OSi_8bit_z19	68.3%	82.0%	45.9%	58.8%
OP_OSi_24bit_z19	86.8%	84.6%	82.1%	83.3%
OP_OSi_8bit_z20	65.3%	70.9%	40.6%	51.6%
OP_OSi_24bit_z20	84.0%	85.0%	72.4%	78.2%

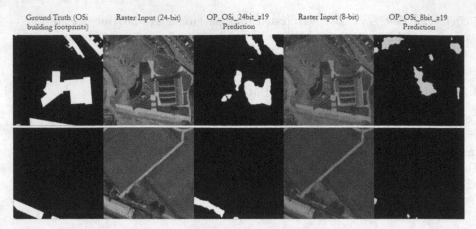

a)   Comparison of predictions from model trained with 30cm/pixel dataset

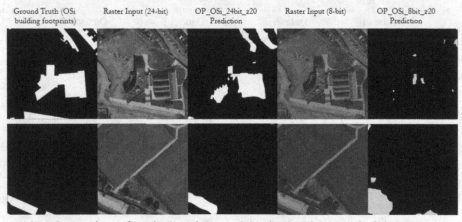

b)   Comparison of predictions from model trained with 15cm/pixel dataset

Fig. 4. Predictions of OSM-GAN model trained with OSi Orthophotos and building footprints.

Figure 4 qualitatively compares the outcomes of the above-listed OSM-GAN model predictions. It can be seen in Fig. 4a that the OP_OSi_24bit_z19 model gives comparatively more accurate results, demonstrating the importance of a qualitative analysis of testing. For example, the OP_OSi_8bit_z20 model predicted a large building that could be identified as an "extension" to existing OSi vector data by the subsequent change detection process.

3.2 Modelling OSM-GAN with OSi-OSM Data

The second experiment was designed to investigate the consistency/coherence between OSi Orthophotos and OSM vectors. Apart from a difference in the spatial reference system used, it was observed that current OSM vectors of the test area are outdated. Therefore, many data samples were filtered out in the data filtering phase. Table 4 summarises the generated datasets using OSi Orthophoto images and OSM vectors.

Table 4. Details of datasets employed in OSi-OSM experiments.

	Dataset 1	Dataset 2	Dataset 3	Dataset 4
Raster source	OSi orthophotos			
Vector source	OSM building footprints			
Resolution	30 cm (*z19*)		15 cm (*z20*)	
Bit-depth	8-bit	24-bit	8-bit	24-bit
Number of samples	641	641	1993	1993
Model ID	OP_OSM_8bit_z19	OP_OSM_24bit_z19	OP_OSM_8bit_z20	OP_OSM_24bit_z20

A quantitative analysis of the testing results is listed in Table 5. In this case, the model trained with a 30 cm (*z19*) 8-bit dataset showed the highest accuracy, while the first experiment produced a model trained on RGB images as the most accurate; in both cases with the same resolution.

Table 5. Quantitative results of the OSi-OSM experiment.

Model ID	Accuracy	Precision	Recall	F1 score
OP_OSM_8bit_z19	76.4%	58.7%	67.3%	62.71%
OP_OSM_24bit_z19	72.1%	63.4%	70.8%	66.90%
OP_OSM_8bit_z20	50.6%	52.0%	55.4%	53.65%
OP_OSM_24bit_z20	20.2%	47.3%	61.9%	53.62%

Figure 5 illustrates the qualitative comparisons of the models in Table 5. Since visual comparisons show only two random instances taken from the test dataset, the visual results perhaps do not support well the quantitative measurements obtained above. However, to improve the change detection workflow, the results should be accurate both quantitatively and qualitatively.

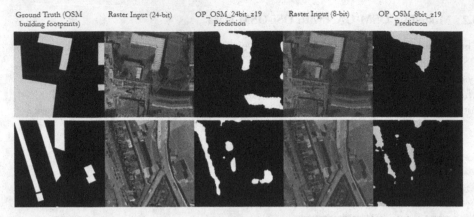

Ground Truth (OSM building footprints)   Raster Input (24-bit)   OP_OSM_24bit_z19 Prediction   Raster Input (8-bit)   OP_OSM_8bit_z19 Prediction

a) Comparison of predictions of the model trained with 30cm/pixel dataset

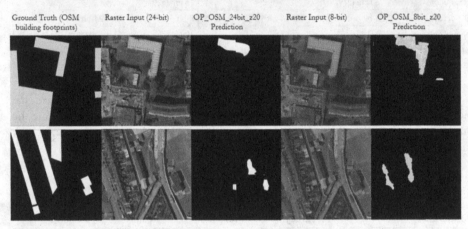

Ground Truth (OSM building footprints)   Raster Input (24-bit)   OP_OSM_24bit_z20 Prediction   Raster Input (8-bit)   OP_OSM_8bit_z20 Prediction

b) Comparison of predictions of the model trained with 15cm/pixel dataset

Fig. 5. Qualitative analysis of predictions from the model trained with OSi Orthophotos and OSM building footprints.

3.3   Modelling OSM-GAN with Google-OSi Data

Models with Google Earth satellite images and OSi building footprints were trained in a third experiment. Four datasets were created using different spatial resolutions and bit-depths. A relatively small AoI fitting OSi boundary constraints was applied to the Google Earth image crawler to collect the relevant satellite images or the area. Table 6 summarises the details about these datasets.

Table 6. Details of the datasets that used in the Google-OSi experiments.

	Dataset 1	Dataset 2	Dataset 3	Dataset 4
Raster source	Google earth satellite images			
Vector source	OSi building footprints			
Resolution	30 cm (*z19*)		15 cm (*z20*)	
Bit-depth	8-bit	24-bit	8-bit	24-bit
Number of samples	644	644	2110	2110
Model ID	Google_OSi_8bit_z19	Google_OSi_24bit_z19	Google_OSi_8bit_z20	Google_OSi_24bit_z20

Table 7 lists the quantitative measurements calculated for the trained models. A model trained with 15 cm RGB images scored better quantitative results than the other three models. After comparing to previous experiments (OSi-OSi and OSi-OSM), the model trained with higher resolution images is quantitatively more accurate.

Table 7. Quantitative results obtained from experiments conducted with Google-OSi datasets

Model ID	Accuracy	Precision	Recall	F1 score
Google_OSi_8bit_z19	66.7%	48.7%	30.6%	37.6%
Google_OSi_24bit_z19	83.0%	68.0%	71.2%	69.56%
Google_OSi_8bit_z20	71.9%	66.6%	62.1%	64.2%
Google_OSi_24bit_z20	85.4%	75.80%	81.10%	78.36%

Figure 6 shows a qualitative comparison of some prediction samples. The predictive results of the Google_OSi_24bit_z20 model (Fig. 6b) agree with the above quantitative results. The predicted polygons can be used in the subsequent change detection process since they are allied to ground truth polygons.

3.4 Modelling OSM-GAN with Google-OSM Data

Finally, yet importantly, Google Earth satellite images and OSM vectors were combined to perform another training phase. Since both data resources are free and unlimited, a wider AoI was chosen and crawled to create the following datasets.

The above-listed datasets were used to train four OSM-GAN models. These models were then evaluated using the same accuracy measurements such as Accuracy, Recall, Precision, and F1 Score (Table 9). The model trained with 30 cm RGB Google Earth satellite images and OSM vector footprints performed better. Significantly, this is the most accurate OSM-GAN model obtained when compared to all the models evaluated in the four experiments.

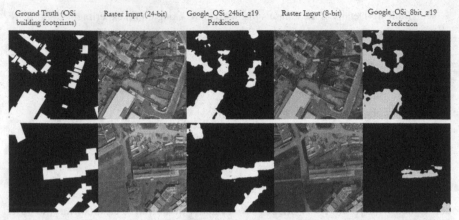

Ground Truth (OSi building footprints) · Raster Input (24-bit) · Google_OSi_24bit_z19 Prediction · Raster Input (8-bit) · Google_OSi_8bit_z19 Prediction

a)   Comparison of predictions of the model trained with 30cm/pixel dataset

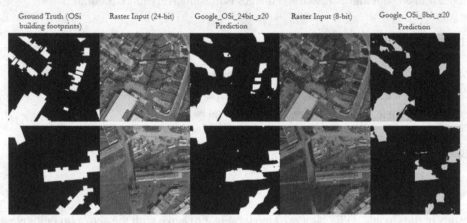

Ground Truth (OSi building footprints) · Raster Input (24-bit) · Google_OSi_24bit_z20 Prediction · Raster Input (8-bit) · Google_OSi_8bit_z20 Prediction

b)   Comparison of predictions of the model trained with 15cm/pixel dataset

Fig. 6. Predictions of models trained with Google Earth satellite images and OSi buildings.

Table 8. Details of datasets used in Google-OSM experiment.

	Dataset 1	Dataset 2	Dataset 3	Dataset 4
Raster source	Google earth satellite images			
Vector source	OSM building footprints			
Resolution	30 cm (z19)		15 cm (z20)	
Bit-depth	8-bit	24-bit	8-bit	24-bit
Number of samples	644	644	2110	2110
Model ID	Google_OSM_8bit_z19	Google_OSM_24bit_z19	Google_OSM_8bit_z20	Google_OSM_24bit_z20

Table 9. Quantitative measurements obtained from the final experiment.

Model ID	Accuracy	Precision	Recall	F1 score
Google_OSM_8bit_z19	86.7%	59.3%	78.1%	67.4%
Google_OSM_24bit_z19	88.4%	62.0%	80.5%	70.0%
Google_OSM_8bit_z20	35.2%	45.8%	61.3%	52.4%
Google_OSM_24bit_z20	68.0%	50.4%	53.7%	52.0%

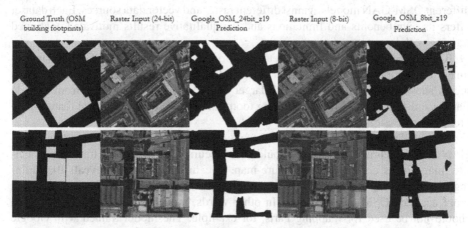

a)   Comparison of predictions of the model trained with 30cm/pixel dataset

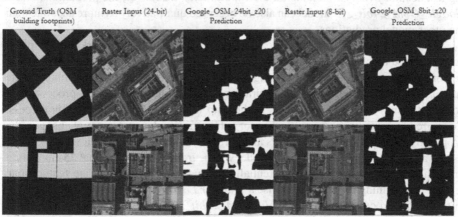

b)   Comparison of predictions of the model trained with 15cm/pixel dataset

Fig. 7. Qualitative comparisons of models trained with Google Earth satellite images and OSM building footprints.

Figure 7 qualitatively compares the prediction results of models trained with Google Earth satellite images and OSM building footprints. In this case, the prediction results of Google_OSM_24bit_z19 shows the best qualitative test result, agreeing with the quantitative results above. Comparing all 16 models tested, the results of model Google_OSM_24bit_z19 suggests to train 30 cm Google Earth satellite images with OSM vector data to obtain the most accurate OSM-GAN models for change detection.

4   Conclusions

This paper presented sixteen different OSM-GAN based experiments with a quantitative analysis of each model produced, as well some qualitative observations. It evaluated different OSM-GAN models against different raster and vector data sources. Each dataset offers its own benefits and limitations and the qualitative results motivated continued training with larger area datasets.

The study concludes that the vector footprint generated by OSM-GAN image-to-image translation could be extended to spatial change detection procedures. Experiments show that model training with larger datasets (i.e. datasets built from Google Earth satellite images and OSM building footprints) yielded more accurate feature-map predictions.

Since the proposed spatial change detection methodology is highly based on OSM-GAN model accuracy, the model should be as accurate as possible to translate a satellite image to its corresponding feature-map. The final experiment reveals that training on larger sets of geographically similar areas could be a solution to generating more accurate OSM-GAN models. In other words, models trained with Dublin data should not be used for mapping Paris, for example. The model trained with Google Earth satellite images (24-bit, 30 cm/pixel) and OSM building footprints scored the highest accuracy (88.4%) among all the experiments. Moreover, the predictions of the *Google_OSM_24bit_z19* model can also be observed qualitatively as more accurate than the other model predictions.

The ultimate objective of this research is to build an end-to-end workflow to update crowdsourced maps automatically with the use of freely available data (satellite images, vector footprints) and Artificial Intelligence (AI) techniques. Automated map update success ultimately depends on the accuracy of the ML change detection process since correctly identifying spatial changes in the map is an initial key step in this process. Compared to contemporary approaches for automatically detecting spatial changes, the proposed OSM-GAN approach offers an appropriate mechanism to follow.

As a next step, a new OSM-GAN model will be trained on the original 25 cm Dublin orthophotos with a larger AoI to potentially produce even more accurate feature-map results. The training process will utilise a *Transfer Learning* approach and so begins by initiating the process using the *Google_OSM_24bit_z19* model parameters as the base input model. In order to evaluate the performance and accuracy of OSM-GAN against other spatial change detection models in the literature, a new test phase will also be carried out on the *crowdAI Mapping Challenge* dataset[3] in future work.

---

[3] https://www.crowdai.org/challenges/mapping-challenge.

Acknowledgements. The authors wish to thank all contributors involved with the OpenStreetMap project. This research is funded by Technological University Dublin College of Arts and Tourism, SEED FUNDING INITIATIVE 2019–2020. The authors wish to acknowledge the Irish Centre for High-End Computing (ICHEC) for the provision of computational facilities and support. We also gratefully acknowledge Ordinance Servey Ireland for providing both raster and vector data for the experiments.

References

1. OpenStreetMap. https://www.openstreetmap.org. Accessed 22 Sept 2021
2. Niroshan, L., Carswell, J.D.: OSM-GAN: using generative adversarial networks for detecting change in high-resolution spatial images. In: 5th International Conference on Geoinformatics and Data Analysis (ICGDA 2022), Paris, France, January 2022, Springer Lecture Notes on Data Engineering and Communications Technologies (2022)
3. Overpass API. https://wiki.openstreetmap.org/wiki/Overpass_API. Accessed 29 Oct 2021
4. Kay. https://www.ichec.ie/about/infrastructure/kay. Accessed 15 Sept 2021
5. What is bit depth? https://etc.usf.edu/techease/win/images/what-is-bit-depth/. Accessed 15 Oct 2021
6. Gong, M., Su, L., Jia, M., Chen, W.: Fuzzy clustering with a modified MRF energy function for change detection in synthetic aperture radar images. IEEE Trans. Fuzzy Syst. **22**(1), 98–109 (2013)
7. Yousif, O., Ban, Y.: Improving urban change detection from multitemporal SAR images using PCA-NLM. IEEE Trans. Geosci. Remote Sens. **51**(4), 2032–2041 (2013)
8. Ronneberger, O., Fischer, P., Brox, T.: U-Net: convolutional networks for biomedical image segmentation. In: Proceedings of the International Conference on Medical Image Computing and Computer-Assisted Intervention, Munich, Germany, 5–9 October 2015, pp. 234–241 (2015)
9. Badrinarayanan, V., Kendall, A., Cipolla, R.: SegNet: a deep convolutional encoder-decoder architecture for image segmentation. IEEE Trans. Pattern Anal. Mach. Intell. **39**, 2481–2495 (2017)
10. SegNet. https://mi.eng.cam.ac.uk/projects/segnet/. Accessed 20 Sept 2021
11. He, K., Gkioxari, G., Dollár, P., Girshick, R.: Mask R-CNN. In: Proceedings of the IEEE International Conference on Computer Vision, Venice, Italy, 22–29 October 2017, pp. 2961–2969 (2017)
12. Isola, P., Zhu, J.Y., Zhou, T., Efros, A.A.: Image-to-image translation with conditional adversarial networks. In: Proceedings of the 2017 IEEE Conference on Computer Vision and Pattern Recognition (CVPR), Honolulu, HI, USA, 21–26 July 2017, pp. 5967–5976 (2017)
13. Image-to-Image Translation with Conditional Adversarial Networks. https://phillipi.github.io/pix2pix/. Accessed 20 Sept 2021
14. Tiecke, T.G., et al.: Mapping the World Population One Building at a Time. arXiv 2017, arXiv:cs/1712.05839
15. Iglovikov, V., Seferbekov, S.S., Buslaev, A., Shvets, A.: TernausNetV2: fully convolutional network for instance segmentation. In: Proceedings of the Conference on Computer Vision and Pattern Recognition Workshops (CVPRW), Salt Lake City, UT, USA, 18–22 June 2018, vol. 233, p. 237 (2018)
16. Microsoft/USBuildingFootprints.   https://github.com/microsoft/USBuildingFootprints. Accessed 20 Sept 2021

17. Zhou, L., Zhang, C., Wu, M.: D-LinkNet: LinkNet with pretrained encoder and dilated convolution for high resolution satellite imagery road extraction. In: Proceedings of the 2018 IEEE/CVF Conference on Computer Vision and Pattern Recognition Workshops (CVPRW), Salt Lake City, UT, USA, 18–22 June 2018, pp. 192–1924 (2018)

18. Oehmcke, S., Thrysøe, C., Borgstad, A., Salles, M.A.V., Brandt, M., Gieseke, F.: Detecting hardly visible roads in low-resolution satellite time series data. arXiv 2019. arXiv:1912.05026

19. Buslaev, A., Seferbekov, S.S., Iglovikov, V., Shvets, A.: Fully convolutional network for automatic road extraction from satellite imagery. In: Proceedings of the Conference on Computer Vision and Pattern Recognition Workshops (CVPRW), Salt Lake Cit, UT, USA, 18–22 June 2018, pp. 207–210 (2018)

20. Xia, W., Zhang, Y.Z., Liu, J., Luo, L., Yang, K.: Road extraction from high resolution image with deep convolution network—a case study of GF-2 image. In: Multidisciplinary Digital Publishing Institute Proceedings, MDPI: Basel, Switzerland, vol. 2, p. 325 (2018)

21. Wu, S., Du, C., Chen, H., Xu, Y., Guo, N., Jing, N.: Road extraction from very high resolution images using weakly labeled OpenStreetMap centerline. ISPRS Int. J. Geo-Inf. **8**, 478 (2019)

22. Xia, W., Zhong, N., Geng, D., Luo, L.: A weakly supervised road extraction approach via deep convolutional nets based image segmentation. In: Proceedings of the 2017 International Workshop on Remote Sensing with Intelligent Processing (RSIP), Shanghai, China, 19–21 May 2017, pp. 1–5 (2017)

23. Sun, T., Di, Z., Che, P., Liu, C., Wang, Y.: Leveraging crowdsourced GPS data for road extraction from aerial imagery. In: Proceedings of the IEEE Conference on Computer Vision and Pattern Recognition, Long Beach, CA, USA, 16–20 June 2019, pp. 7509–7518 (2019)

24. Ruan, S., et al.: Learning to generate maps from trajectories. In: Proceedings of the AAAI Conference on Artificial Intelligence, New York, NY, USA, 7–8 February 2020

25. Albert, A., Kaur, J., Gonzalez, M.C.: Using convolutional networks and satellite imagery to identify patterns in urban environments at a large scale. In: Proceedings of the 23rd ACM SIGKDD International Conference on Knowledge Discovery and Data Mining, Halifax, NS, Canada, 13–17 August 2017, pp. 1357–1366 (2017)

26. Rakhlin, A., Davydow, A., Nikolenko, S.I.: Land cover classification from satellite imagery with U-Net and Lovasz-Softmax loss. In: Proceedings of the Conference on Computer Vision and Pattern Recognition Workshops (CVPRW), Salt Lake City, UT, USA, 18–22 June 2018, pp. 262–266 (2018)

27. Cao, R., et al.: Integrating aerial and street view images for urban land use classification. Remote Sens. **10**, 1553 (2018)

28. Kuo, T.S., Tseng, K.S., Yan, J.W., Liu, Y.C., Wang, Y.C.F.: Deep aggregation net for land cover classification. In: Proceedings of the Conference on Computer Vision and Pattern Recognition Workshops (CVPRW), Salt Lake Cit, UT, USA, 18–22 June 2018, pp. 252–256 (2018)

29. Schmidhuber, J.: Unsupervised minimax: adversarial curiosity, generative adversarial networks, and predictability minimization. arXiv 2019, arXiv:cs/1906.04493

30. Albrecht, C.M., et al.: Change detection from remote sensing to guide OpenStreetMap labeling. ISPRS Int. J. Geo Inf. **9**(7), 427 (2020)

31. Lebedev, M.A., Vizilter, Y.V., Vygolov, O.V., Knyaz, V.A., Rubis, A.Y.: Change detection in remote sensing images using conditional adversarial networks. International Archives of the Photogrammetry, Remote Sensing & Spatial Information Sciences, 42(2) (2018)

32. Papadomanolaki, M., Verma, S., Vakalopoulou, M., Gupta, S., Karantzalos, K.: Detecting urban changes with recurrent neural networks from multitemporal Sentinel-2 data. In: IGARSS 2019–2019 IEEE International Geoscience and Remote Sensing Symposium, pp. 214–217. IEEE, July 2019

Tourists Preferred Streets Visualization Using Articulated GPS Trajectories Driven by Mobile Sensors

Iori Sasaki[✉], Masatoshi Arikawa, Ryo Sato, and Akinori Takahashi

Graduate School of Engineering Science, Akita University, Akita 010-8502, Japan
sasaki@lab.akita-u.info

Abstract. Although there has been a lot of research on GPS big data analysis to discover the preferred spots and destinations for tourists, discovering the preferred streets also plays an important role in improving tourism content and optimizing transportation systems. In general, GPS data has inaccuracies and redundancies, and its density is biased to specific locations. This causes difficulty making tourists preferred streets stand out by using density-based visualizations such as heatmaps. In this study, we attempted to apply a mobile sensor-based data cleaning method, which is executed at the end-user device, and thereby equalize the bias of each tourist's trajectory data. This paper examines how to generate a heatmap from such lightweight and non-unstable data and whether it can effectively visualize tourists preferred streets using real tourism data. A heat map was created by plotting GPS data on a geographic grid square and focusing on the quartiles of density values. The results were almost consistent with the tendency of actual tourist routes. The contribution of this research is that it does not require any preparation such as a road network, and does not require a large amount of computation compared to conventional approaches.

Keywords: GPS big data · Tourists preferred streets · Density-based approach · Heatmaps

1 Introduction

In a big data era, various types of data help create understandings of tourist behavior and enhance tourist experiences. Big data used in the fields of tourism can be categorized into UGC (User Generated Content, e.g., text, photos, and audio), device (e.g., GPS and signals from base stations), and transaction (e.g., shopping and accommodation records) [1]. Especially, GPS data has the advantage that you can collect large quantities at a low cost, especially with the spread of smartphones. The most popular example of data mining focusing on GPS data is to detect and predict hot spots (tourists preferred spots) [2, 3]. However, few studies on the detection and prediction of tourists preferred streets, which can be also important for regional tourism development. For example, in the case of walking tourism, a road brimming with cherry blossoms and a street with a historical atmosphere have the potential to attract many people. In addition, if we

© Springer Nature Switzerland AG 2022
F. Karimipour and S. Storandt (Eds.): W2GIS 2022, LNCS 13238, pp. 43–50, 2022.
https://doi.org/10.1007/978-3-031-06245-2_4

know streets taken by many pedestrians, we can optimize development plans of urban landscape and operation schedules of urban buses. Therefore, this study aims to discover streets that attract a lot of attention by using GPS big data. Density-based visualizations using conventional methods of generating heatmaps may be useful to achieve our goal. However, GPS trajectory data collected from tourist users have some characteristics that prevent visualizing tourists preferred streets because of high contrast between staying and moving trajectory data. In this paper, we first clarify factors by using GPS data of actual tourists. Then, we discuss how much our mobile sensor-based data cleaning approach can contribute to generating visualizations that enable hot streets detection.

2 Related Work

In the fields of transportation, there have been studies on traffic analysis and prediction using GPS data for congestion detection [4]. Their basic approaches are map matchings with road networks [5]. However, pedestrians have higher degrees of freedom of movement than automobiles. Therefore, these are very cost-intensive businesses for our research questions.

Some approaches are using *Euclidean distance* and *Dynamic time warping* to measure the similarity of trajectory shapes and detect frequently used routes. However, tourists preferred streets are often a part of sightseeing routes for them, and it is pointed out that the computational complexity is still too large to handle a large number of GPS trajectories [6].

GPS data mining using clustering methods based on point cloud density (e.g., kNN query [7] and DBSCAN [8]) can be found for hot spot (stay point) detections [9]. GPS trajectory data of tourists, who tend to stay in the same place for a while, are less affected in detections of hot spots. On the other hand, regarding tourists preferred streets, as the number of sample data increases, hot areas become difficult to recognize.

From the above discussion, it is necessary to reduce the cost of preparation and computation in order to deal with a large amount of universal GPS data. In this paper, we will study how to improve the existing density-based approach to realize a visualization that makes the existence of streets more prominent.

3 Heatmap-Based Approaches

3.1 Heatmap Generation of GPS Data

A heatmap is a data visualization technique that presents each value on a certain two-dimensions by using multiple colors or gradation. Readers can understand data patterns and distributions through it intuitively. In this paper, we present geographical grid-based heatmaps. The specific generation method is as follows. First, a target geospatial area is divided into a 10 m × 10 m square grid. Then, we plot sample data. The number of GPS data in each grid $g(s, t)$ is counted, and a score table is generated. Finally, the second quartile and the third quartile of the score table (Q_2, Q_3) are calculated, and the color of each grid is determined based on Fig. 1.

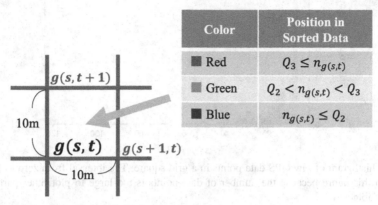

Color	Position in Sorted Data
■ Red	$Q_3 \leq n_{g(s,t)}$
■ Green	$Q_2 < n_{g(s,t)} < Q_3$
■ Blue	$n_{g(s,t)} \leq Q_2$

Fig. 1. Rules for assigning color in each grid square. $n_{g(s,t)}$ is the number of recorded points in a square $g(s, t)$.

3.2 Difficulty in Visualizing Streets and Paths

We investigated why heatmaps are not suitable for detecting streets and paths by using twelve sample datasets. The sample data was collected in Akita City by having twelve subjects carry a cell phone (Apple Inc.'s Phone 11). They walked freely around the city using a guide map published by Akita City. GPS data is automatically recorded at 15-s intervals.

Figure 2 and 3 show a density (the number of points in each mesh) distribution of the twelve trajectories data and a heatmap generated according to Sect. 3.1. At the center and the upper left part of the heat map, round-shaped red areas are drawn. In general, tourists often stay for a while in several facilities during their travel. This means that GPS trajectories of tourists tend to have some parts containing many points within a small area. In addition, since the accuracy of GPS reception gets significantly lower indoors, many points with large errors are recorded there. These factors lead to dense and scattered points in a trajectory.

In addition, places where people have paused for traffic lights or taking breaks and parts where walking speed is slow tend to be hot areas. Therefore, these cause that the existence of streets is overshadowed by hot spots because the data bias gets larger as the number of samples increases.

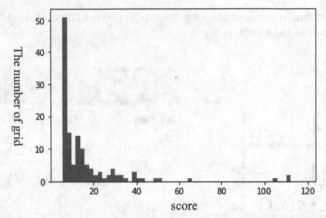

Fig. 2. A histogram of raw GPS data points in a grid square. The interval from zero to five are omitted in this figure because the number of data points is too large to plot other parts in an understandable way.

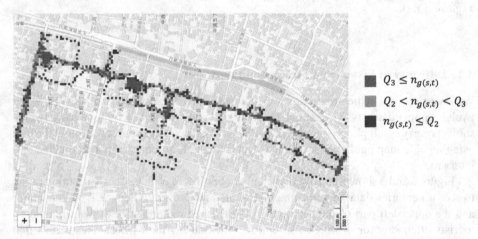

$Q_3 \leq n_{g(s,t)}$

$Q_2 < n_{g(s,t)} < Q_3$

$n_{g(s,t)} \leq Q_2$

Fig. 3. A heatmap using raw trajectory data. It is ambiguous to clarify where are significant paths for tourists.

4   Solutions to Unclearness of Hot Paths by Data Articulation

4.1   Street-Detectable Heatmap Generation

Considering the problems of heatmap approaches, it would be a feasible solution to make distributions of each trajectory homogeneous for generating street-detectable heatmaps. To mitigate the redundancy of GPS trajectories, reducing sampling rate and/or applying existing line simplification algorithms would be useful. However, the former can lose correspondence between a trajectory and a base map, and the drawing is no longer called walkers' route. The latter is not enough to eliminate dense noises that are unique to GPS trajectories. Then, we propose to apply the Multiple Mobile Sensor-Based Articulation

(MMSBA), which we have proposed so far, to this research. MMSBA was originally developed for enriching user experiences of a digital diary that you browse through GPS logs on maps. It is a method that mitigates the redundancy and inaccuracy of GPS trajectory data by using a combination of data such as acceleration and GPS horizontal accuracy estimates that can be obtained from smartphones. It is one of purposes of this paper to verify whether the trajectory data generated through MMSBA, a data cleaning method executed in the side of end users, play a useful role in tourist behavior analysis. However, processed trajectory data themselves cannot be used for heatmap generation because it retains only the minimum number of reference points for trajectory drawing and loses geographical continuity. The conceptual diagram of the street-detectable heatmaps generation is shown in Fig. 4.

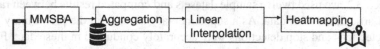

Fig. 4. The conceptual diagram of the street-detectable heatmaps generation.

4.2 Multiple Mobile Sensor-Based Articulation (MMSBA)

MMSBA is a method to efficiently mitigate the redundancy of GPS data by using a combination of mobile sensor data. It combines three key methods, that is, (A) an *Inside Detection* method using GPS accuracy values, (B) a *Stop Detection* method using acceleration values, and (C) an existing *line simplification* algorithm (Douglas-Peucker Algorithm [10]) to generate trajectories with significantly reduced point clouds [11]. The following gives a brief explanation of the first two methods.

- Inside Detection

When a user is indoors, the values of GPS accuracy data decrease because of ceilings and walls. That is why unstable and unreliable trajectories are drawn around there. To solve this problem, we used GPS horizontal accuracy data and threshold method to judge indoors and abstracted them into a point by calculating the center point of their minimum bounding box. The research set 10.0 m to the threshold. Furthermore, we introduced tolerant distance buffering that makes our inside detection more robust. (1) Recorded points from the time when the threshold is exceeded until it is lowered again are defined as a provisional indoor segment. (2) A midpoint of the minimum bounding box of points in the segment is calculated. (3) The system starts to monitor the distance between the midpoint and the user's location. (4) If you are judged to be indoor again before the distance exceeds the tolerant distance, points in the segment are regarded as continuous outdoor points and back to (2). (5) If the distance exceeds the tolerant distance, an indoor segment is determined.

• Stop Detection

When a tourist is stationary for a while, such as waiting for a traffic light to change, a messy line is drawn. To solve this problem, we used acceleration data to detect "walk-ing" and "stopping" states and removed the outdoor stationary points as redundant parts. Modern mobile devices such as smartphones and tablets can collect three-axis accelera-tion values. Our research deals with a square root of the sum of the squares of them as a raw value and applies a low-pass filter to reduce the sensor noise. Then, you can obtain intuitive changes of acceleration values with low latency (less than 100 ms).

5 Results and Discussion

As in Sect. 3.2, we used twelve sample datasets and compared results between raw GPS data and articulated GPS data. As a supplementary note, from the preliminary survey, inside detections and stop detections were accurately conducted in these data. Figure 5 and 6 show a density distribution of the twelve articulated trajectory data and a heatmap generated according to Fig. 4.

Looking at the histogram (Fig. 5), extremely dense areas disappear compared to the histogram of the raw data (Fig. 2). In addition, the scattering condition of values is also smaller, indicating that the effects of staying indoors and stopping for a while are suppressed. Next, you can recognize that the heatmap (Fig. 6) shows a continuous red line. The results are almost consistent with the actual tourist behavior. More than 90% of the data used in this study is collected from students in their early twenties, and we have not been able to conduct experiments that take into account user attributes and means of transportation. In actual environments, moving speeds varies from person to person. However, our method is expected to be less susceptible to differences in sampling rate and moving speed, because we applied uniform articulation and linear interpolation to all GPS trajectory data.

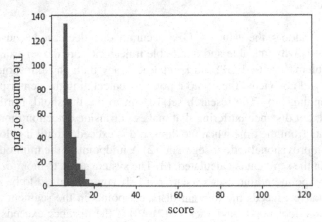

Fig. 5. A histogram of data points of articulated GPS trajectory in a grid square. The interval from zero to five are omitted in this figure because the number of data points is too large to plot other parts in an understandable way.

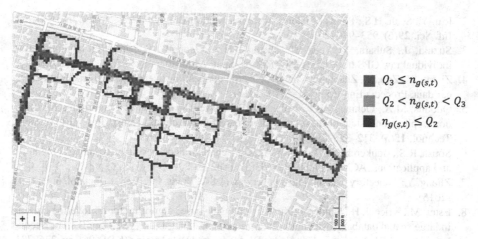

$Q_3 \leq n_{g(s,t)}$

$Q_2 < n_{g(s,t)} < Q_3$

$n_{g(s,t)} \leq Q_2$

Fig. 6. A heatmap using trajectory data becomes cleaner after the processing through the proposed method MMSBA.

6 Conclusion

We examined problems and approaches in visualizing tourists preferred streets using user trajectory big data in this paper. As tourism styles become more diverse, tourists come to use a variety of means of transportation for their activities. Hence, an approach that does not require the cost of road networks is necessary. However, GPS data with a lot of redundancy can be difficult to detect streets. We attempted to homogenize the distribution of GPS trajectory data and highlight hot streets by using MMSBA, a data cleaning approach using multiple mobile sensors. According to our results, articulated trajectories can successfully visualize the existence of them and have a possibility of achieving the research goal.

This study used twelve sample datasets, and it is necessary to increase the amount of data for the next stage. It is difficult to use existing datasets such as GeoLife [12] because MMSBA also focuses on mobile data that has not been dealt with in previous research in the fields of GPS trajectory cleaning. Therefore, we are currently preparing for the release of a walking tour application and building a system to collect our own datasets.

Acknowledgments. The authors would like to thank Akita City for providing the fascinating illustrated maps and content of the walking tours. We are also grateful to the subjects that participated in our user experiments. This research were supported partly by JSPS KAKENHI Grant Numbers JP19K20562 and JP19H04120.

References

1. Li, J., Xu, L., Tang, L., Wang, S., Li, L.: Big data in tourism research: a literature review. Tour. Manage. **68**, 301–323 (2018)

2. Liu, Y., Seah, H.S.: Points of interest recommendation from GPS trajectories. Int. J. Geogr. Inf. Sci. **29**(6), 953–979 (2015)
3. Suzuki, J., Suhara, Y., Toda, H., Nishida, K.: Personalized visited-POI assignment to individual raw GPS trajectories. ACM Trans. Spat. Algorithms Syst. **5**(3), 1–28 (2019)
4. Zhang, Y., Zuo, X., Zhang, L., Chien, Z.: Traffic congestion detection based on GPS floating-car data. Procedia Eng. **15**, 5541–5546 (2011)
5. Quddus, M.A., Ochieng, W.Y., Noland, R.B.: Current map-matching algorithms for transport applications: state-of-the art and future research directions. Transp. Res. Part C Emerg. Technol. **15**(5), 312–328 (2007)
6. Sousa, R.S., Boukerche, A., Loureiro, A.A.F.: Vehicle trajectory similarity: models, methods, and applications. ACM Comput. Surv. **53**(5), 1–32 (2020)
7. Zheng, Y.: Trajectory data mining: an overview. ACM Trans. Intell. Syst. Technol. **6**(3), 1–41 (2015)
8. Ester, M., Kriegel, H., Sander, J., Xu, X.: A density-based algorithm for discovering clusters in large spatial databases with noise. In: Simoudis, E., Han, J., Fayyad, U. (eds.) The Second International Conference on Knowledge Discovery and Data Mining (KDD-96), pp. 226–231. AAAI Press (1996)
9. Schneider, C., Gröchenig, S., Venek, V., Leitner, M., Reich, S.: A framework for evaluating stay detection approaches. ISPRS Int. J. Geo Inf. **6**(10), 315 (2017)
10. Douglas, H.D., Peucker, T.K.: Algorithms for the reduction of the number of points required to represent a digitized line or its caricature. Cartographica Int. J. Geograph. Inf. Geovisualization **10**(2), 112–122 (1973)
11. Sasaki, I., Arikawa, M., Takahashi, A.: Articulated trajectory mapping for reviewing walking tours. ISPRS Int. J. Geo Inf. **9**(10), 610 (2020)
12. Zheng, Y., Xie, X., Ma, W.: GeoLife: a collaborative social networking service among user, location and trajectory. IEEE Data Eng. Bull. **33**(2), 32–39 (2010)

Constructing Place Representations from Human-Generated Descriptions in Hebrew

Tal Bauman[1] , Itzhak Omer[2] , and Sagi Dalyot[1]

[1] Mapping and Geo-Information Engineering, Civil and Environmental Engineering Faculty, The Technion, Haifa, Israel
{talbauman,dalyot}@technion.ac.il
[2] Department of Geography and Human Environment, Tel Aviv University, Tel Aviv-Yafo, Israel
omery@tauex.tau.ac.il

Abstract. Space is a natural and indispensable part of the human communication form, mostly based on natural-spatial descriptions with varying lexical structures that rely on human spatial cognition and perception. This is a "geographic language" which machines do not understand, and accordingly do not properly process. Consequently, geographic information retrieval is limited due to the lack of rich and comprehensive textual-geographical databases required, for example, for spatio-query processes. While in English there exists a relatively rich set of libraries and tools, in Hebrew there is a void, with no automatic tools for addressing this problem. We propose a methodology that mimics human literal place descriptions, utilizing implicit geometries and topologies existing in geospatial databases. This study focuses on the first stage, which includes collecting a lingual dataset of human place descriptions with an online survey. Using Hebrew Natural Language Processes, place entities and their spatial relations were extracted from the survey descriptions. Similar place entities and relations were simultaneously extracted from OpenStreetMap database. Through place queries that rely on textual phrases from these two sources, human descriptions of places were geolocated. Finally, these locations were compared to retrieved locations acquired through Google maps API on survey descriptions - showing very promising results in accurately locating the described places.

Keywords: Geographic information retrieval · Hebrew · Natural language processing · Human spatial cognition

1 Introduction

Geographic Information Retrieval (GIR) encompasses numerous scientific and engineering challenges, most of which are derived from the lack of rich and comprehensive spatio-textual databases needed to carry out the process. Until recently, the used textual databases were manually tagged for a place or location (Gazetteer). The aspiration nowadays is to be able to analyze and understand various human-related phenomena using GIR algorithms for, e.g., georeferencing text in a mechanized way [1]. GIR processes present various complex and demanding scientific and engineering challenges, where

© Springer Nature Switzerland AG 2022
F. Karimipour and S. Storandt (Eds.): W2GIS 2022, LNCS 13238, pp. 51–60, 2022.
https://doi.org/10.1007/978-3-031-06245-2_5

various approaches and techniques are developed that present spatial context without being explicitly linked to a defined location. Current methods are mostly based on text databases, in which text-entities are manually referenced (tagged) with predefined locations [2]. These databases are often characterized by poor and homogeneous knowledge and spatial discontinuities [3], thus deriving limited and non-generic capabilities [4, 5]. Consequently, current GIR processes are not structured to comprehensively consider human spatial perception and description of place, particularly in Hebrew. English, for example, presents simple morphology, and as such can be processed with automatic annotation pipelines, while Hebrew is a morphologically rich language, so similar pipelines limit the applicability for text analysis [6].

This study focuses on the investigation, analysis and generation of an enriched geospatial database that will also store spatio-textual labels on the places and geographic features it stores. To do this, we examine an "inverted" approach that automatically computes spatio-textual linguistic descriptions from existing geographic and geospatial databases and linking them to specific geographic features (places). Geographic databases mostly contain a structured and continuous description of the spatial information on which geographical knowledge is built. Such that certain descriptions are inherently expressed in the geometric representation of entities in space - entities that are associated with certain attributes (accompanying tabular information), as well as the topological relations between the entities [7]. To compute this type of linguistic descriptions in a textual configuration, thus digitally mimicking the human cognitive-linguistic process, the verbal "building blocks" commonly used for human spatial description are explored and formulated. Algorithms that allow automatic computation of specific geotags from untagged geospatial databases are developed to support the process. Such an enriched database holds great potential for building and institutionalizing complex GIR processes, and for further research on aspects associated with human spatial perception. This work-in-progress provides preliminary missing knowledge and proposes algorithms to allow enhanced GIR in Hebrew to enable complex and qualitative geographic queries.

2   Methodology

2.1   Online Survey

To obtain natural human place descriptions, an online survey[1] was structured that included 30 known places in Tel-Aviv, depicted in Table 1 and Fig. 1. Tel-Aviv is the second largest city in Israel, constituting an important financial, cultural, and commercial hub and the center of the largest metropolitan area in Israel. Tel Aviv has a grid-like streets network with north oriented imageable main streets, which helps residence to navigate and communicate [8]. The selected places come from a variety of place types, including 6 squares, 8 compounds, 3 markets, 7 buildings, 3 parks, 2 neighborhoods and one bridge. The assumption is that due to their differences, e.g., type, geometry, and context, they will produce diverse human generated textual descriptions to constitute a heterogeneous dataset. These places represent urban objects of different function and experience as well as various urban image elements, for example: district (neighborhood

---

[1] http://wize-web.com/GIR/Default.html (in Hebrew).

and compounds), landmark (buildings and parks), path (bridge), and node (squares). As such, they can generate cognitive representations and place descriptions at different scales, reference frames and spatial knowledge types.

Table 1. Places used in the survey.

ID	Place Name	Type	Area [m^2]
1	Rabin Square	Square	30,812
2	Tel Aviv University	Compound	579,787
3	Jaffa Port	Compound	119,180
4	Pishpeshim market	Market	76,490
5	New Tel Aviv central bus station	Building	20,747
6	Levinsky market	Market	130,354
7	Neve Tzedek	Neighborhood	371,822
8	Charles Clore Park	Park	116,689
9	Great Synagogue of Tel Aviv	Building	4,739
10	Shuk HaCarmel	Market	39,266
11	Kerem HaTeimanim	Neighborhood	119,174
12	TLV Fashion Mall	Building	7,666
13	Yehudit bridge	Bridge	4,037
14	Sarona	Compound	102,285
15	HaKirya	Compound	221,875
16	Habima Square	Square	32,370
17	Bialik Square	Square	1,559
18	Meir Park	Park	25,932
19	Dizengoff Center	Building	26,422
20	Dizengoff Square	Square	9,854
21	London Ministores Tower	Building	7,983
22	Azrieli Towers	Building	43,972
23	Masaryk Square	Square	4,893
24	Ichilov Hospital	Compound	105,032
25	Terminal 2000 - Bus Terminal	Compound	85,855
26	Hamedina Square	Square	88,399
27	Tel Aviv Port	Compound	170,389
28	Hayarkon Park	Park	780,247
29	Reading Power Station	Building	373,492
30	Gordon Beach	Compound	90,389

For the online survey, the respondents inserted their age, gender, education level, and place of residence, allowing us to explore the relationships between places by groups of people [9]. After the respondent submits these details, the place names are shown one by one in increasing order in terms of existing count of descriptions per place in the dataset. For each place, the respondent is asked whether she/he is familiar with it, and if so, she/he is asked to describe in free text the place for a person who does not know it - without explicitly naming the place in the text. Each respondents answers two questions: where the place is located, and what can be seen in it. The online survey included 239 respondents providing 1,271 textual place descriptions. The respondents were asked to describe at least 5 places with at least 4 words each.

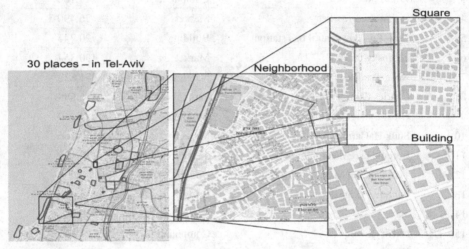

Fig. 1. The 30 chosen places in Tel Aviv, depicted in red polygons (left), with zoom-in areas (middle and right).

2.2 Geographic Layers to Vector Space

Based on descriptions and bag-of-words identified from the survey, the 10 most frequently used terms are investigated. OpenStreetMap (OSM) was used to build the initial description database, mainly since it is open source, containing various vernacular geographic information with updated street networks and points of interest (POIs). According to the used bag-of-words and terms in the textual descriptions, we focused on the various topological relations of the places to the street network, namely: main streets (as defined by OSM road type), intersections (junctions) and directionality (azimuth). Accordingly, the textual descriptions of streets topology, such as streets intersection, between streets, streets absolute direction, are computed based on OSM data and attached to the entity data (place) stored in OSM. With this method, other descriptions can be later added from supplementary data represented as POIs and polygon layers.

The city of Tel Aviv was divided into 1,708 blocks based on OSM's street network layer by using the road type tag that equals to 'primary'. A function was developed to extract the streets that surround each block, separating them into two groups: intersected and parallel streets, depicted in Fig. 2. The streets' name and their relations to other streets (for example: intersection) was calculated and marked with predefined characters (symbols). In IR terminology, these characters are termed tokens, whereas here, the tokens are used to symbolize the relative description of a block by the relevant streets in terms of intersections, directions, and relative relations.

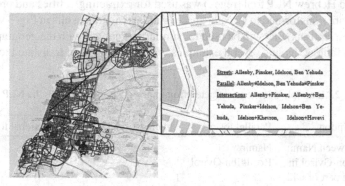

Fig. 2. 1,708 blocks in Tel Aviv (left). Example of one block with tokenization metadata (right): parallel streets marked with # and intersections marked with +.

At the end of this process, each block is associated (and tokenized) with the streets that surround it, their corresponding topology, its relations with other streets that fall inside it, and the relative directions to primary roads. Figure 3 depicts the binary form of these blocks - white for 'False' (no tokenization exists) and black for 'True' (a specific tokenization exists), where the rows represent the blocks, and the columns represent the used tokens. Accordingly, the geographic layers in OSM are transformed into a vector space that will be used for similarity analysis with the textual queries.

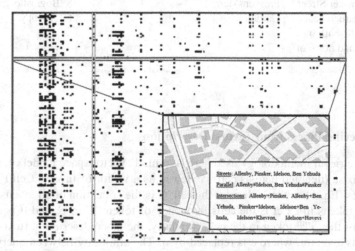

Fig. 3. Binary representation of a sample of the formulized database. Rows – blocks; Columns – tokens. In orange, the token "west to Namir Street" is presented.

2.3   Textual Place Descriptions to Vector Space

This process aims to transform the 'free text place descriptions' that were collected in the online survey into a 'binary token' representation. The first stage includes filtering punctuation from all descriptions and creating a dictionary of all terms. The second stage handles the extraction of entities (to this end – only street names) and the prepositions. For both, a basic Hebrew NLP tool (regex) was used for extracting entities and prepositions. The results are transformed to a vector space (similarly to the results in Fig. 3 where rows are place descriptions) that will be used for similarity analysis with the geographic layers (Sect. 2.4). Table 2 depicts several examples of token extraction translated to English.

Table 2.   Example of tokens extracted from place descriptions using the NLP tool.

Place description	Parallel tokens	Intersection tokens	Directional tokens
Located between Namir Road and Ibn-Gvirol in the northern part of Old Tel Aviv	Namir Road#Ibn-Gvirol	–	–
The intersection of Idelson and Bialik streets	–	Idelson + Bialik	–
Between Begin Road and Ayalon Lanes and Hashalom Road to the south	Begin Road#Ayalon	–	S*Hashalom Road
Located north of Allenby south of Meyer Park and west of King George	–	–	S*Allenby, S*Meyer Park, W*King George
Between Pinsker Street and Meir Garden near the City Hall south of Bograshov and north of Allenby	Pinsker#Meir Garden	–	S*Bograshov, N*Allenby

2.4   Retrieving Places from Textual Descriptions

The place retrieval methodology used here is termed 'Vector space model'. Each block in the database (denoted here as cell) is viewed as a vector of Inverse Cell Frequency (ICF) values (Eq. 1), where c denotes the cell, C is the collection of all tokens, N is the number of tokens in C, cf is the cells frequency of token "i" in C, and tf is the token frequency of the "i"th token in the cell. Similarly, the place description (text query) is described as a vector, where c is replaced by q. The similarity between query (q) and block (c) is measured by a cosine similarity (Eq. 2). With cosine similarity, the cells, in the form of vectors, are sorted in terms of Euclidean distance or angle size compared (matched) to the query (textual descriptions) vector. The smaller the angle, the closer the similarity, i.e., the textual description is analogous to the place. Since each place description is attached to the true reference position (ground-truth), the place retrieval error can be calculated as the place location difference in metric units (distance).

$$\vec{c} = \langle tf(t_i, c) \times icf(t_i, C) \rangle = \left\langle tf(t_i, c) \times \log\left(\frac{N}{cf(t_i, C)}\right)\right\rangle \tag{1}$$

$$sim(q, c) = \frac{\vec{q} \cdot \vec{c}}{\|q\|\|c\|} = \frac{\sum_{i=1}^{n} q_i c_i}{\sqrt{\sum_{i=1}^{n} q_i^2}\sqrt{\sum_{i=1}^{n} c_i^2}} \tag{2}$$

3   Experimental Results

3.1   Textual Dataset

Figure 4 depicts the distribution of gender, age, and education of all survey respondents, showing an almost equal number of males and females. Most of the respondents are aged 20 to 30 and have graduated from elementary school or have an academic diploma. A third of the respondents live in Tel Aviv, which should provide a good starting point to examine local knowledge (i.e., spatial knowledge and understanding acquired by direct experience with the environment) in terms of place descriptions. Although to some extent the respondent population is homogenous, their characteristics distribution still allows us to assess the description type and commonly used words of each group.

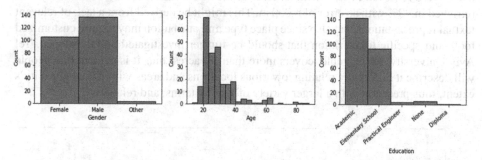

Fig. 4. Respondents' histograms of gender, age, and education (left to right).

3.2   Place Retrieval Analysis

To evaluate the proposed methodology, we compared our process to Google Maps geocoder API[2]. For each textual place description from the online survey, we retrieved the first-place result from Google Maps and our query on the enriched OSM. The location of each retrieved place was compared to the true (known) place location in terms of Euclidean distance (nearest entity node). Figure 5 depicts the distance comparison

---

[2] https://developers.google.com/maps/documentation/geocoding/overview.

results of both retrieval processes in boxplots for all places. The overall results are similar, where in the 90th percentile (top black line), our proposed process presents a better retrieval accuracy of 2,810 m compared to 2,927 m. For the 50th percentile (orange line), Google Maps' retrieval accuracy is better: 309 m compared to 531. Overall, both retrieval processes are similar in terms of identifying the queried place, although our process presents relatively more outliers.

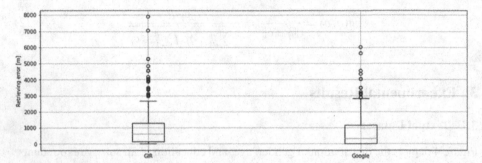

Fig. 5. GIR on OSM and Google Maps geocoder API comparison in terms of distance accuracy.

Figure 6 depicts the retrieval accuracy of all places. In our suggested process (in blue), more than 50% of places were retrieved within less than half a kilometer, which is a very promising error value in terms of the relatively small number of used tokens. For example, TLV mall, London mini-stores and the great synagogue were retrieved in 90% with an error of few meters only. Riding power station and Tel Aviv port, on the other hand, were retrieved in 90% with an error of 3,000 m, where Tel Aviv University was retrieved in 90% with an error of 6,000 m. This might be derived from a lack of relevant textual representations, but also since place type and attribution may require customized tools and specific tokenization that should be further investigated and developed. Tel Aviv University, for example, covers more than 30 acres, thus it is evident that people will describe it differently relating to various locations and areas within the university's extent, thus present it with a larger variety of words, terms, and relations.

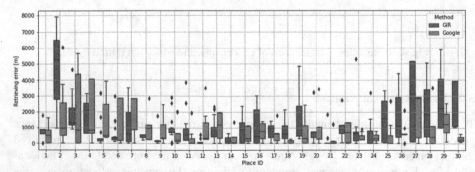

Fig. 6. Place distance retrieval error comparison between Google Maps (orange) and our proposed process (blue) for all places using boxplots. Y-axis depicts the distance error in a resolution of 1000 m, and X-axis depicts the searched place names (respectively to Table 1). (Color figure online)

Figure 7 depicts two place retrieval distance distributions according to the number of used words (left) and place area (right). It is visible that some correlation exists between the number of used words and the retrieval accuracy, where in general longer place descriptions lead to better place retrieval. Similarly, the larger the place area - the lesser the retrieval accuracy (P-value < 0.005).

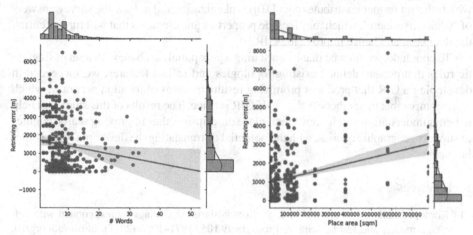

Fig. 7. Place retrieval error according to the correlation of number of used words per description (left) and place size (right).

4 Conclusions and Future Work

In this study, we present the first stages of our methodology to enrich geospatial databases by automatically computing literal descriptions of places with the aim to improve GIR, focusing on Hebrew place text queries. The idea is to digitally mimic the human linguistic by identifying common words and terms used for place description, compute them from existing database relations and indexes, and attach them to the corresponding places as additional attributes. Here, we presented the preliminary survey we conducted to generate the initial bag-of-words and showed the potential of the tokenization and vectorization processes in correctly retrieving the places described in text descriptions. When compared to the commonly used Google Maps geocoder API, our methodology showed promising results in terms of location accuracy.

Our preliminary analysis showed that people use few syllables as possible to describe a place, with a preference for descriptions using names and spatial relations - rather than quantitative geometric indices. Moreover, the use of salient features, such as street names and landmarks, as reference points, and the use of absolute directions are evident in the place text descriptions. Since not much was done in relation to the analysis of Hebrew literal spatial description, it was found that it is similarly structured as other languages (e.g., [8]).

Several new developments should be considered to improve the GIR in terms of place location accuracy. One issue is related to the used dataset, being relatively homogenous (used words and terms) since it was created relying on volunteers who are friends, family, and colleagues; a more heterogenous and wider population is needed. Also, the existing analysis did not consider the different place types, also in terms of their area, that might affect the used words and terms, which requires additional investigation in terms of tokenization to further enrich the database. The existing tokens were created while relying on a limited set of rules, mainly topology, without considering the variety of spatial relations (e.g., scale) and other database elements, such as reference to POIs, which should further contribute (e.g., [10]). Tokenization did not use the survey answers of 'what exists there', which may include properties and elements that will further enrich the database, and hence improve the GIR.

To conclude, we showed that by enriching a geospatial database with a set of linguistic rules that present defined existing topologies and salient features, we succeeded in developing a GIR that produces promising results in terms of location accuracy, which were comparable to another off-the-shelf GIR service. The results of this study can help in better understating the Hebrew literal place description, thus improving search engines to support geographic queries, with the potential of translating the developments to other languages.

References

1. Kordopatis-Zilos, G., Papadopoulos, S., Kompatsiaris, I.: Geotagging text content with language models and feature mining. Proc. IEEE **105**, 1971–1986 (2017). https://doi.org/10.1109/JPROC.2017.2688799
2. Karimzadeh, M., Pezanowski, S., MacEachren, A.M., Wallgrün, J.O.: GeoTxt: a scalable geoparsing system for unstructured text geolocation. Trans. GIS **23**, 118–136 (2019). https://doi.org/10.1111/tgis.12510
3. Zhu, D., et al.: Understanding place characteristics in geographic contexts through graph convolutional neural networks. Ann. Am. Assoc. Geogr. **110**, 408–420 (2020). https://doi.org/10.1080/24694452.2019.1694403
4. Kordopatis-Zilos, G., Papadopoulos, S., Kompatsiaris, Y.: Geotagging social media content with a refined language modelling approach. In: Chau, M., Wang, G., Chen, H. (eds.) PAISI 2015. LNCS, vol. 9074, pp. 21–40. Springer, Cham (2015). https://doi.org/10.1007/978-3-319-18455-5_2
5. Gritta, M., Pilehvar, M.T., Limsopatham, N., Collier, N.: What's missing in geographical parsing? Lang. Resour. Eval. **52**(2), 603–623 (2017). https://doi.org/10.1007/s10579-017-9385-8
6. Tsarfaty, R., Seker, A., Sadde, S., Klein, S.: What's Wrong with Hebrew NLP? And How to Make it Right. arXiv preprint arXiv:1908.05453 (2019)
7. Wang, L., Zhang, F., Du, Z., Chen, Y., Zhang, C., Liu, R.: A hybrid semantic similarity measurement for geospatial entities. Microprocess. Microsyst. **80**, 103526 (2021). https://doi.org/10.1016/j.micpro.2020.103526
8. Omer, I., Jiang, B.: Imageability and topological eccentricity of urban streets. In: Jiang, B., Yao, X. (eds.) Geospatial Analysis and Modeling of Urban Structure and Dynamics, pp. 63–175. Springer, Berlin (2010)
9. Yuan, X., Crooks, A., Züfle, A.: A thematic similarity network approach for analysis of places using volunteered geographic information. ISPRS Int. J. Geoinf. **9**, 385 (2020). https://doi.org/10.3390/ijgi9060385
10. Hu, Y., Adams, B.: Harvesting big geospatial data from natural language texts. In: Werner, M., Chiang, Y.-Y. (eds.) Handbook of Big Geospatial Data, pp. 487–507. Springer, Cham (2021). https://doi.org/10.1007/978-3-030-55462-0_19. ISBN 978-3-030-55461-3

Optimising Antenna Positioning for Maximum Coverage: The Case Study of Cattle Tracking in Austrian Alps Using Long Range (LoRa) Based Monitoring System

Franz Welscher[1], Rizwan Bulbul[1(✉)], Johannes Scholz[1(✉)], and Peter Lederer[2]

[1] Institute of Geodesy, Graz University of Technology, Graz, Austria
franz.welscher@student.tugraz.at, {bulbul,johannes.scholz}@tugraz.at
[2] ViehFinder, St. Radegund, Austria
peter.lederer@viehfinder.com
https://ifg.tugraz.at/ , https://viehfinder.com/

Abstract. This paper presents an approach to solve the antenna coverage location problem (ACLP) in the context of tracking cattle in the Austrian Alps. In cooperation with ViehFinder a process is determined for optimizing the placement of the antennas using a DEM with a resolution of 1m. The paper identifies several constraints, such as mobile reception, proximity to a street and a maximum slope, that influence the number of candidate positions. Further, the demand nodes are restricted to the alp areas. Of the possible objectives for the ACLP, such as (1) complete coverage, (2) maximum coverage with a budget and (3) backup coverage, this paper focuses on maximizing the coverage in respect to a given budget. The optimization model discussed here uses visibility analyses to determine the viewsheds - i.e. the covered area - of the antennas and Integer Linear Programming (ILP) to solve the locational problem of placing the antennas. It will be applied to two study areas. The first study area is located near Graz in Styria containing about 277.3 million candidate positions and demand points. The second is close to the western border of Carinthia and consists of 47.5 million demand nodes and possible candidate locations. Due to the size of the problem computational problems might result, when using ILP. Therefore the use of genetic algorithms and heuristics is considered as well. Especially NSGA-II that has been suggested as one of the viable solutions for problems of similar nature and complexity. The sheer size of the problem is unprecedented, thus future work will explore the boundaries of the proposed approach.

Keywords: Antenna coverage location problem · Spatial optimization · Viewshed analysis · Cattle mobility · LoRa · LoRaWAN

The project is partially funded by Steirische Wirtschaftsförderungsgesellschaft m.b.H.

F. Karimipour and S. Storandt (Eds.): W2GIS 2022, LNCS 13238, pp. 61–70, 2022.
https://doi.org/10.1007/978-3-031-06245-2_6

1   Introduction

Alpine farming is an important aspect of agriculture in the Austrian mountain regions. These permanent grassland areas not only contribute to an attractive cultural landscape, but are also vital for securing the biodiversity in the alpine regions [2]. There are about 8,000 alpine pastures with a forage area of 311,000 ha. With 301,000 cattle, 50,000 cows and other animals such as sheep, horses or goats, it is a huge part of farming in the Austrian mountains [4].

Livestock farming is an important part of agriculture not only in Austria but has become one of the fastest-growing sectors of agriculture globally due to the rapid growth in population and expansion of urban areas [23]. Movement and forage intake of the livestock is most likely to affect and be affected by the ecosystems surrounding it. Thus parameters such as vegetation growth dynamics, wildlife behaviour and demographics, and disease transmissions affect livestock farming. The mobility of cattle can be monitored using modern positing systems (both GNSS and non-GNSS based systems and techniques) and can provide vital information to farmers, land managers and conservationists to make informed decisions [25].

One company that provides a solution for tracking cattle on the Alps is ViehFinder. The solution uses Long-Range (LoRa) radio frequency antennas and solar powered GNSS based collars for the cattle to transmit the position of the cattle and temperature of the environment to the server every 10 min. The proposed system enables the near real-time monitoring of the cattle alerting farmers in case the cattle leaves their property (geofencing) or shows any unusual behaviour (predator attack). The stored mobility and environmental data is supposed to be analyzed in a variety of ways. For example, extensive spatio-temporal analysis of the mobility data can be performed to enable farmers to make informed decisions on the management of their alps [14–16].

Effective monitoring of cattle using ViehFinder's proposed solution needs the extensive coverage of the area of interest with a sufficient number of antennas. However, the unit cost of an antenna is 1,260€ and makes up the major chunk of the ViehFinder hardware setup [17]. In order to make the solution viable for farmers, it is needed that the minimum numbers of antennas are installed while maximizing the coverage area of these antennas. We'll later refer to this as Antenna coverage location problem (ACLP).

This work in progress paper proposes an approach to optimize the number and coverage of the antennas using spatial optimization techniques. Visibility analysis [24] and coverage models, such as maximum coverage location problem (MCLP) [6] are used to solve the problem at hand. At the end a procedure for determining the optimal positions of the antennas based on an input digital-elevation-model (DEM) and constraints for antenna positioning will be developed. Thus the model has to satisfy certain objectives and constraints that occur when tracking cattle in remote areas. The primary research question this paper faces is:

- Can the problem of optimal antenna positions for monitoring cattle movement in alpine regions be modeled with spatial optimization techniques?

Further questions that are addressed in the paper are:

- Which constraints determine the antenna candidate positions?
- Which algorithmic techniques can be used to improve the optimization process?

In Sect. 2 this paper will introduce the ViehFinder system, which can be used to track cows in the alps. Further a review of locational problems is conducted and the Antenna coverage location problem is introduced, as an equivalent of the Maximal Covering Location Problem. Section 3 presents the study areas and the constraints of the problem. Section 4 shows the proposed solution, as well as the tools that are used. It also gives insight into first results and other tools that must be considered. Finally, Sect. 5 concludes this paper with a discussion and a differentiation of the ACLP from similar problems.

2   Background

2.1   ViehFinder

ViehFinder is an integrated solution for animal tracking in remote areas. With the focus on robust devices and energy self-sufficient components, it allows a maintenance-free operation and allows unprecedented high time resolution of positioning data. ViehFinder consists of two hardware components (Fig. 1) and one software component. The ViehFinder node, which is a Long-Range (LoRa®) based sensor unit with a GNSS module. It is typically fixed on a collar and mounted around the neck of animals, e.g. cattle or other livestock. In addition, it contains an acceleration sensor and a temperature probe which allows the tracking of special animal behavior and the environmental conditions. The energy source is a 0.5 W solar module with an attached Lithium-Polymer (LiPo) battery cell installed, which allows continuous operation of the node. The second component is the LoRaWAN (Long Range Wide Area Network) antenna. It receives the sensor signals from the ViehFinder nodes and routes the signals with a LoRaWAN Gateway and a connected cellular router via the Internet to the data storage and data processing servers. Due to the range restrictions, and since the data connection between node and antenna can only be guaranteed in direct line-of-sight, there might be more than one antenna required for a defined area, which needs to be covered. Thus the optimal positioning of these antennas is the focus of this work.

The third part, the ViehFinder control server, contains the essential software components to operate the system. It needs a controller software that features the collection and pre-processing of tracking data. This system is implemented based on Node.js and Node-RED. It also features a time series data platform for the storage and retrieval of the sensor data. This component is implemented with InfluxDB, a cloud database for handling real-time temporal data.

Fig. 1. Two components of the ViehFinder setup, solar powered ViehFinder node (left) and LoRaWAN antenna (right).

2.2 Locational Problems (LP)

Locational problems are spatial optimization problems that determine optimal locations of facilities that need to provide a certain coverage. A classical example are fire stations that need to cover a city. In particular, if one would define that neighborhoods need to be covered in a way that they are not more than 5 driving minutes away from the next fire station - often having limited resources. Hence, the planning of new fire stations is a complex computational task that requires mathematical modeling and optimization techniques. De Smith et al. [8] compiled a taxonomy of locational problems that lists the components and the basic classes of locational problems accordingly. According to De Smith et al. [8], "cover" can be defined and modeled using a variety of metrics ranging from Euclidean distance, line-of-sight, to service time.

Church and Murray [7] define three different classes of locational problems:

- Location Set Covering Problem (LCSP) [26]
- Maximal Covering Location Problem (MCLP) [6]
- Minimum Impact Location Problem (MILP) [20]

The LCSP minimizes the number of facilities required to cover a demand area in a way that the maximum service time/distance is still guaranteed [26] - and the whole area is covered by the service. The MCLP [6] is based on the LCSP, but does not guarantee a complete service coverage over the whole area of interest. Furthermore, the MCLP uses a given amount of resources, and tries to find the maximum (i.e. best) coverage with respect to the bounded resources. The MILP [20] is a formulation of a spatial optimization problem that seeks to locate facilities in a way that their impact on neighboring entities is minimal - such as nuclear power plants.

2.3 Antenna Coverage Location Problem (ACLP)

ACLP is a coverage location problem concerned with the optimal placement of a minimum number of antennas (transmitters or receivers or both) to achieve maximum coverage. MCLP is a non-deterministic polynomial time (NP)-hard optimization problem thus ACLP is one as well and depending on the size of the problem it might only be solvable using heuristic approaches [1,19]. There are several approaches to solve ACLP using mathematical programming languages like ILP, heuristics, metaheuristics, and evolutionary algorithms. Some papers also use Machine Learning in combination with evolutionary algorithms to solve this problem [1,9,21]. There are several possible scenarios for the ACLP in this case. (1) The farmer wants to have the alp covered completely, which would require the LSCP. (2) The farmer works with a budget and can only afford a certain number of antennas leading to the usage of the MCLP. (3) A certain amount of backup coverage is needed, requiring demand points to be covered by more than one antenna. Either way it is necessary to compute the viewshed of each candidate position which returns all locations in the area that can be seen from the position within a specified distance [24]. Viewshed might be a simplification of the spread of radio frequencies, but covered areas and areas of radar shadow can be determined [18]. Further coverage of a collar through an antenna can only be guaranteed, when it lies in the line of sight. For the ACLP each pixel of the DEM of a given Area of Interest (AoI) is considered a demand point that needs to be covered by an antenna. A pixel is considered covered, when it lies within the viewshed of a candidate position. The viewshed of each antenna depends on its height, range and the surrounding area. In general placing antennas on a hilltop will yield better viewsheds, than placing them in a valley. Although there is only a low correlation between visibility and elevation, because a peak can be surrounded by other peaks impairing its viewshed [13]. S. Bao et al. [3] faced a similar problem, when trying to optimize fire watchtower locations. The major difference between the positioning of the watchtowers and the antennas in this paper, is that in this case there are no given candidate positions. Each pixel of the DEM that fulfills certain constraints is considered a potential antenna position. The following section explains requirements, constraints and challenges that arise, when dealing with such a mutable number of candidate positions.

3   Requirements and Challenges

Two study areas are chosen for developing and testing the proposed procedure as shown in Fig. 2. The first one is the test area Schöcklland reaching from the outer borders of Graz to Weiz in Styria, Austria. It covers a total of $277.34\,km^2$, thus it contains about 277.3 million demand points and possible candidate positions, when using a DEM with 1 m resolution. The second study area is located in the upper Mölltal and is $47.55\,km^2$ that's only about one fifth of the first area's size. Yet it still has 47.5 million demand points and candidate positions. Thus it is vital for the computation time to reduce the number of demand points and the potential antenna locations.

Furthermore, the computation of the viewsheds requires the height and range properties of the antennas, as well as the coordinates of the candidate position.

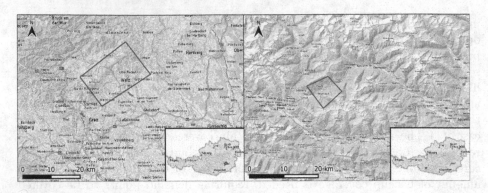

Fig. 2. Overview maps of the two study areas. Study area Schöckelland in Styria (left) and study area Upper Mölltal in Carinthia (right).

As mentioned, the proposed antenna uses LoRa-radio frequency technology and has a range of 8 km [16]. The antenna can be placed at different heights. For this project a general height of 2 m is assumed. The coordinates are taken from each candidate pixel of the DEM. There are several requirements that restrict the number of possible antenna locations. (1) Easy access for the installation and maintenance of the antenna is important, thus a candidate position has to be within a range of 100–200 m of the next street. (2) Another aspect, also concerning the accessibility, is that the slope is below 20%–30%, excluding difficult terrain. (3) The third and last constraint is the reception of a mobile network, because otherwise the antenna can't send the tracking data to the server. The street data can be acquired from OpenStreetMap (OSM), the slope can be calculated from the DEM and the mobile network coverage is provided by the BMLRT [5].

Concerning the demand points the area of the alps in the study area is used. Thus excluding all pixels that are not part of an alp. Although a buffer of 200 m around the alp areas is included, because the cattle should still be trackable in case animals leave the farmer's property.

Finally, the MCLP needs the number of allowed antenna positions or rather a budget for selecting the antenna positions that provide the best coverage. For example, this constraint can be given as 6,000€ allowing the algorithm to place 4 antennas with a price of 1,260€ each.

The biggest challenge for this project was mentioned at the beginning of this section. Handling the immense number of candidate positions and demand points is a tough task and requires a lot of computational power. Especially achieving a solution in a reasonable amount of time is complex but important for the real-world usage of ViehFinder project.

4   Proposed Solution

The procedure proposed in this paper for solving the ACLP can be seen in Fig. 3. The figure shows that at the beginning the demand points and candidate points are generated from the relevant data sets. The demand points are gained from clipping the DEM with the cadastre areas and converting it to vector points. The candidate positions however result from applying the three constraints, mobile network coverage, proximity to a street and maximum slope to the DEM. For each candidate position a viewshed is computed, which leads to as set of viewsheds that are handed to the optimization tool Allagash with the demand points. As a result it returns the optimal viewsheds.

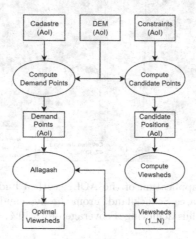

Fig. 3. Spatial optimization approach depicting the relevant inputs and processes. Describes steps from the raw data at the beginning to the optimized output at the end.

Once the candidate positions are determined their viewsheds are computed and handed to the python optimization module Allagash [22] along with the demand points. Allagash uses GeoPandas in combination with PuLP to model the spatial optimization problems LSCP and MCLP [22]. We then use the Coin-or Branch and Cut integer programming solver that comes along with PuLP to solve the problem [12]. Because most farmers are restrained by a budget, covering their complete area might not be feasible for them. For that reason, this paper focuses on the application of the MCLP in the context of this scenario. Therefore, the objective function for this problem reads as follows:

$$\sum_{j=1}^{N} with Z_j = \begin{cases} 1 & \text{if cell j is covered by at least one antenna} \\ 0 & \text{otherwise} \end{cases}$$

For now it just tries to maximize the number of covered demand points for a set of possible antenna positions. Future objectives are covering the complete area with a minimum amount of antennas, as well as providing a certain amount of backup coverage in case of the failure of an antenna.

Figure 4 is an example for the problem at hand and shows the alp areas surrounding St. Radegund bei Graz (47.18°N, 15.49°E) together with five manually set antenna candidate positions. These antenna locations could potentially cover 54.24% of the alp area in the region. Running the MCLP with a maximum of 3 antennas returns the antennas 1, 2 and 3 as optimal and achieves a total coverage of 42.30%.

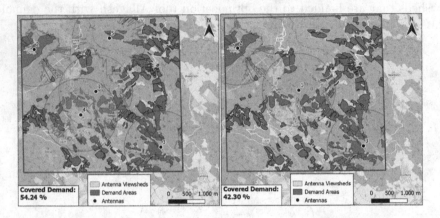

Fig. 4. Example for the application of the ACLP with a budget of 3 antennas on a small subset of the study area Schöcklland. From the five candidate positions 1, 2 and 3 are chosen as optimal, thus achieving a coverage of 42.30%.

Initial test runs were executed on a HP notebook with an i7 with 2.6 GHz and 16 GB of RAM. The largest data set run so far consisted of 100,000 demand points and 1000 candidate positions. In total it took about 3 h and 42 min to receive the optimal solution. Further improvements of the algorithm show promising results, but benchmark runs are still to be made.

We are aware that the sheer size of the problem, might lead to computational problems, when using ILP. For that reason, we have alternative solutions in mind such as using the genetic algorithms, especially NSGA-II that has been suggested as one of the viable solutions for problems of similar nature and complexity. Heyns et al. [11] for example used it for solving about 46000 candidate positions.

5   Discussion and Future Prospects

This paper proposes an approach for solving ACLP for monitoring cattle mobility using spatial optimization. Literature suggests many approaches for the ACLP in diverse domains such as wildfire detection. Some of the proposed solutions can handle large problem instances but to the best of our knowledge none of those can handle millions of demand points and antenna candidate positions. Thus the major difference between previous work and our approach is the context and the sheer size of the problem.

Having this high degree of freedom in the placement of the antennas and the large amount of demand points leads to a challenging computational burden. Reducing the number of candidate positions and demand points through the mentioned constraints might not be enough. There are several ways of further filtering them. Heyns et al. [10], for example, use a geomorphological approach to restrict candidate positions to hills and ridges. Heyns [10] uses a reduced target-resolution strategy to reduce demand points uniformly. Therefore, a similar approach might be needed for the problem at hand.

Another way of choosing antennas could be setting a threshold for their minimum coverage. That means that a candidate position with a viewshed that covers less than the threshold is skipped. For example, if the threshold is set to 50%, then all antennas that cover less area than 50% of the possible 100% are skipped. Future work on this project will explore the boundaries of modelling optimal antenna positions in alpine regions with spatial optimization models. We evaluate different optimization approaches - ranging from exact to heuristic methods - for the given problem size and complexity.

Furthermore, we will evaluate antenna constraints for their usefulness and their influence on the problem size, complexity and computational time. The same goes for the demand points constraints.

References

1. Amiri, F.: Optimization of facility location-allocation model for base Tranceiver station antenna establishment based on genetic Algorithm considering network effectiveness criteria (case study North of Kermanshah). Scientia Iranica **0**(0), 0 (2021). https://doi.org/10.24200/sci.2021.55207.4116
2. BABF, BMLFUW: Almstatistik 2009, September 2010. http://www.berggebiete. eu/cm3/de/themen/berglandwirtschaft/547-ff43-almstatistik-2009.html
3. Bao, S., Xiao, N., Lai, Z., Zhang, H., Kim, C.: Optimizing watchtower locations for forest fire monitoring using location models. Fire Saf. J. **71**, 100–109 (2015). https://doi.org/10.1016/j.firesaf.2014.11.016
4. BMLRT: Grüner Bericht 2021. Die Situation der österreichischen Land- und Forstwirtschaft. Technical report (2021). https://gruenerbericht.at/cm4/ jdownload/download/2-gr-bericht-terreich/2393-gb2021
5. BMLRT, RTR-GmbH, WIGeoGIS-GmbH, Geoland.at, AMA: Breitbandatlas (2021). https://breitbandatlas.gv.at/
6. Church, R., ReVelle, C.: The maximal covering location problem. Pap. Reg. Sci. **32**(1), 101–118 (1974)
7. Church, R.L., Murray, A.: Location Covering Models. ASS, Springer, Cham (2018). https://doi.org/10.1007/978-3-319-99846-6
8. De Smith, M.J., Goodchild, M.F., Longley, P.: Geospatial Analysis: A Comprehensive Guide to Principles, Techniques and Software Tools. Troubador Publishing Ltd. (2007)
9. Dreifuerst, R.M., et al.: Optimizing coverage and capacity in cellular networks using machine learning. In: ICASSP, IEEE International Conference on Acoustics, Speech and Signal Processing - Proceedings 2021-June, pp. 8138–8142 (2021). https://doi.org/10.1109/ICASSP39728.2021.9414155

10. Heyns, A.M.: Reduced target-resolution strategy for rapid multi-observer site location optimisation. IEEE Access **8**, 203252–203269 (2020). https://doi.org/10.1109/CCESS.2020.3037025. https://ieeexplore.ieee.org/document/9253553/
11. Heyns, A.M., du Plessis, W., Curtin, K.M., Kosch, M., Hough, G.: Decision support for the selection of optimal tower site locations for early-warning wildfire detection systems in South Africa. Int. Trans. Oper. Res. **28**(5), 2299–2333 (9 2021). https://doi.org/10.1111/itor.12928
12. Johnjforrest et al.: coin-or/Cbc: Version 2.10.5 (32020). https://doi.org/10.5281/ZENODO.3700700
13. Kim, Y.H., Rana, S., Wise, S.: Exploring multiple viewshed analysis using terrain features and optimisation techniques. Comput. Geosci. **30**(9–10), 1019–1032 (2004). https://doi.org/10.1016/j.cageo.2004.07.008
14. Lederer, P.: ViehFinder. Aktuelle Situation (2021). https://viehfinder.com/der-berg-ruft/
15. Lederer, P.: ViehFinder. Digitale Alm (2021). https://viehfinder.com/digitale-alm/
16. Lederer, P.: ViehFinder. Produkte. (2021). https://viehfinder.com/produkte-preise/
17. Lederer, P.: ViehFinder. ViehFinder Preiskalkulator (2021). https://viehfinder.com/preiskalkulator/
18. Łubczonek, J.: Application of GIS techniques in VTS radar stations planning. In: 2008 Proceedings International Radar Symposium, IRS, pp. 1–4 (2008). https://doi.org/10.1109/IRS.2008.4585766
19. Marianov, V., ReVelle, C.: Siting Emergency Services. Facility Location, pp. 199–223 (1995). https://doi.org/10.1007/978-1-4612-5355-6_11
20. Murray, A.T., Church, R.L., Gerrard, R.A., Tsui, W.S.: Impact models for siting undesirable facilities. Pap. Reg. Sci. **77**(1), 19–36 (1998)
21. Porras, C., et al.: Internet of things and artificial intelligence 2019 a fuzzy multi-objective maximal covering location problem for Wi- Fi antennas location. Contact Information (2019)
22. Pulver, A.: Allagash (2020). https://apulverizer.github.io/allagash/
23. Robinson, T.P., et al.: Mapping the global distribution of livestock. PLoS ONE **9**(5) (2014). https://doi.org/10.1371/journal.pone.0096084
24. Sander, H.A., Manson, S.M.: Heights and locations of artificial structures in viewshed calculation: how close is close enough? Landscape Urban Plann. **82**(4), 257–270 (2007). https://doi.org/10.1016/j.landurbplan.2007.03.002
25. Schieltz, J.M., Okanga, S., Allan, B.F., Rubenstein, D.I.: GPS tracking cattle as a monitoring tool for conservation and management. Afr. J. Range Forage Sci. **34**(3), 173–177 (7 2017). https://doi.org/10.2989/10220119.2017.1387175
26. Toregas, C., Swain, R., ReVelle, C., Bergman, L.: The location of emergency service facilities. Oper. Res. **19**(6), 1363–1373 (1971)

Efficient Multiscale Representations for Geographical Objects

Nieves R. Brisaboa, Alejandro Cortiñas, Pablo Gutiérrez-Asorey$^{(\boxtimes)}$,
Miguel R. Luaces, and Tirso V. Rodeiro

Universidade da Coruña, CITIC, Database Lab. Elviña, 15071 A Coruña, Spain
{nieves.brisaboa,alejandro.cortinas,pablo.gutierrez,
miguel.luaces,tirso.varela.rodeiro}@udc.es

Abstract. Maps need different representations of the same cartographic object in order to display it at several scale levels. When a user zooms in, the object should depict every detail as it is the main focus on the map. On the contrary, when the user zooms out, there is no need to display every single detail of the object as most would become as small as to be invisible. A common technique to speed up the display process is storing several representations for the same object at different scales. However, this technique raises redundancy, and therefore it increases space usage. This work aims at suppressing that redundancy by introducing four alternatives that use a unique representation for each cartographic object while still being able to retrieve simplified versions of them depending on the requested scale.

Keywords: Cartographic generalization · Compression · Geographical information systems

1 Introduction

Cartographic generalization is a process in which a given representation of a geographical object is simplified in order to produce a less detailed version of the same object adequate to be seen at a certain scale [6]. For example, on a map that aims at representing the outline of the full European continent, there is no need to depict every single nook of the coast. However, if the map just covers the northern coast of Spain, even the smallest peninsula may be of interest. Sending simpler versions of cartographic objects cheapens transmission costs without an apparent loss of quality. On the other hand, simplified versions of the map are cheaper to process, therefore it is of interest to have such simplified versions

This work was supported by the CITIC research center funded by Xunta/FEDER-UE 2014–2020 Program grant ED431G 2019/01. Partially funded by MCIU-AEI/ FEDER-UE [BIZDEVOPS: RTI2018-098309-B-C32]; by MICINN (PGE/ERDF) [EXTRA-Compact: PID2020-114635RB-I00; MAGIST: PID2019-105221RB-C41; SIGTRANS-UDC: PDC2021-120917-C21; FLATCITY-POC: PDC2021-121239-C31]; by Xunta de Galicia/FEDER-UE [GRC: ED431C 2021/53].

F. Karimipour and S. Storandt (Eds.): W2GIS 2022, LNCS 13238, pp. 71–81, 2022.
https://doi.org/10.1007/978-3-031-06245-2_7

in order to show them when the scale of the map does not need much detail. These smoother variants of the objects can be obtained through cartographic generalization algorithms. A cartographic generalization algorithm is one that takes a complex, fully-detailed, representation of a geographical object as its input, and outputs a less detailed representation of the same object [6]. The recursive application of such an algorithm would provide increasingly lesser-detailed representations of the original object, as illustrated in Fig. 1. There are several techniques of cartographic generalization: aggregation, reclassification, simplification, etc. A good survey can be found at [7]. Out of all these, line simplification is one of the simplest and widely used methods, being the Douglas-Peucker [2] algorithm the most popular approach.

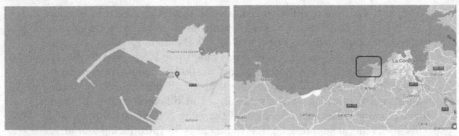

(a) Outline of a port at 1:500 scale   (b) Outline of the port at 1:2000 scale.

Fig. 1. An example of geometry generalization in practice taken from Google Maps. A port is displayed with all details when the user zooms in (left) but the port is reduced to a simple sketch when the user zooms out (right).

In modern GIS applications, different representations of the objects obtained from cartographic generalization are stored separately. Hence, the system can quickly send the requested objects for any given level of scale (zoom).

Storing several representations of the same geographical object at different levels of detail generates a vast volume of redundant information as every point of an object displayed at a certain scale would be included again at every more detailed scale, as exemplified in Fig. 2. Observe how the level with the least amount of detail (denoted in the image as *level 1*) does not include the point (x_2, y_2). However, every successive level does, as well as all the points already contained in Level 1. The last level (*level N*), corresponding with the representation of the full geometry, contains all the points.

This work aims to design and implement new approaches to efficiently store and manage multiple representations of the same object by addressing the inherent redundancy of state-of-the-art solutions. We introduce in the following sections four alternatives, all of them reducing more than 85% the storage space compared to the traditional representation of an object geometry for each scale level. Our promising results are due to two reasons: more efficient approaches to store the raw data using compression techniques, and the complete elimination

Full geometry = [(x_1,y_1), (x_2,y_2), (x_3,y_3), (x_4,y_4), (x_5,y_5), (x_6,y_6), (x_7,y_7), (x_8,y_8), (x_9,y_9) ..., (x_{n-2},y_{n-2}), (x_{n-1},y_{n-1}), (x_n,y_n)]

Level 1 = [(x_1,y_1),	(x_4,y_4), (x_5,y_5),	(x_8,y_8),	..., (x_{n-2},y_{n-2}),	(x_n,y_n)]
Level 2 = [(x_1,y_1), (x_2,y_2),	(x_4,y_4), (x_5,y_5), (x_6,y_6),	(x_8,y_8),	..., (x_{n-2},y_{n-2}),	(x_n,y_n)]
		...		
Level N-1 = [(x_1,y_1), (x_2,y_2),	(x_4,y_4), (x_5,y_5), (x_6,y_6), (x_7,y_7), (x_8,y_8),		..., (x_{n-2},y_{n-2}), (x_{n-1},y_{n-1}), (x_n,y_n)]	
Level N = [(x_1,y_1), (x_2,y_2), (x_3,y_3), (x_4,y_4), (x_5,y_5), (x_6,y_6), (x_7,y_7), (x_8,y_8), (x_9,y_9) ..., (x_{n-2},y_{n-2}), (x_{n-1},y_{n-1}), (x_n,y_n)]				

Fig. 2. Multiple representation of the same object at different scales.

of any kind of redundancy. Moreover, we also include, as a proof-of-content, some experimental results demonstrating how our solutions can recover the representation of a geographical object at any given level of detail in a reasonable time compared against a classical relational spatial database (PostgreSQL).

2 Background

2.1 Basic Concepts of GIS Technologies

GIS technologies use one of two primary types of spatial representations: raster and vectorial. The raster model defines a grid where each cell stores the value of a particular spatial property (e.g. elevation, temperature, etc.). In opposition, the vector model stores the geometries of the spatial objects to represent (country borders, rivers, roads, etc.) using the coordinates of its points. The vector model considers three basic elements: points, polylines, and polygons. Point data refers to a single point in space defined by its geographical coordinates (latitude and longitude), whereas a polyline is a concatenation of points in order where each point represents a vertex of the polyline (e.g. a nook in a coast border). Polygons can be thought of as closed polylines, where the first and last points are equal. Line simplification and other cartographic generalization techniques work over the vector model, smoothing lines and polygons by excluding some of their vertices to shape a simplified representation of them.

The coordinate values of each point (longitude and latitude) are usually expressed in decimal degrees. Double-precision values are the standard data type for coordinate values in most GIS applications, as well as web mapping applications. A decimal degree at the equator corresponds roughly to 111 km. This means that, for example, 0.0001° correspond to roughly 11.1 m, whereas 0.00001° correspond to 1.11 m at the equator.

Double-precision values are encoded with 64 bits. To save space, doubles can be converted into integers. The process of transforming doubles to integers is trivial. First, to avoid working with negative values, we also scale all of our data to zero by subtracting the minimum value of each axis from all values on that axis. Then the process consists simply of moving the comma of the double value until it becomes an integer number. This process of offsetting and scaling double values to integer values is common in GIS applications.

The most fundamental query for any GIS user interface is to recover the polylines contained within a bounding box defined by $(x_{max}, y_{max}, x_{min}, y_{min})$. This implies calculating all the intersection points of the object's geometry with the window. Hence, we need to recover all the points in the polyline of the object between those intersection points. For this purpose, we define the operation $res \leftarrow \texttt{retrieve}(ps, pe, lv_i)$ that returns, from the geometry of an object stored as a coordinate sequence (i.e., each point represented by a longitude and latitude value), all the intermediate points stored between any two positions, ps and pe, at a given level of detail lv_i.

2.2 Compressed Data Representation

The constant increase of stored information in almost every discipline has boosted the evolution of new compression techniques that tackle the repetitiveness of the data to reduce their size. In this work, we follow the trail of [1], introducing new original compressed solutions that may serve as alternatives for storing representations of a geographical object at different levels of detail.

To explain our solutions, we need to define a commonly used structure in compression known as bitvector. A bitvector B is a sequence of zeros and ones, i.e. an array of bit values, of a given length n as displayed in Fig. 3. The two basic operations supported by a bitvector are $rank_1$ and $select_1$ [4]. $rank_1(B, p)$ counts the number of ones until a given position p on the bitvector B. By storing counters of the accumulated $rank$ value at at regular intervals, it is possible to support the $rank_1$ operation in constant time ($O(1)$) with just $o(n)$ additional bits for the counters. On the other hand, $select_1(B, n)$ returns the position of the n_{th} 1 on the bitvector B. The $select_1$ operation can be supported by the same auxiliary structure used for $rank_1$ but its time complexity is $O(log_n)$. Note that similar $rank_0$ and $select_0$ operations can be defined.

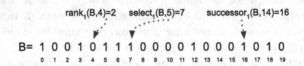

Fig. 3. Bitvector example with rank, select and successor operations.

A more complex operation is $successor_1$ [5]. $successor_1(B, p)$ returns the position of the next 1 on B starting from position p. This operation can be solved with a time complexity of $O(1)$ using the same auxiliary structure for $rank_1$. Again, the same definition would apply for $successor_0$.

Finally, instead of using 32 bits to represent a value in an array of integer values, we can use exactly the number of bits needed for representing the bigger integer, that is, we use $\lceil log_2 M \rceil$ bits, with M being the largest value in the array. This guarantees that the least amount of bits possible for encoding the values is used, gaining compression compared to storing the array as a sequence of 32-bit integers. These implementation improvements can be easily handled by a popular C++ library for efficient data structures [3].

3 Our Proposals

This section introduces four alternatives to represent simplified versions of geographical objects without redundancy.

3.1 Proposal 1: Naive Solution

For our first proposal, we designed a rather simple solution that we call *Naive Solution*. This approach stores the values of both axis (longitude and latitude) in two integer vectors that we will call X and Y. Then, given N levels of detail, it also stores $N-1$ bitvectors of size n, with n being the total number of points that describe the original geometry of the object. For every bitvector a 1 is set at position $B_i[j]$ to indicate that the detail level i includes the point j. Therefore, B_i indicates which points of the full geometry are included in the representation of the level of detail lv_i. The last level lv_N will correspond with the full geometry of the object, hence it will always include all the points, meaning a bitvector B_N will have all its positions set to 1. This makes it unnecessary to store a bitvector for the last level of detail.

Full geometry X $= [x_1, x_2, x_3, x_4, x_5, x_6, x_7, x_8, x_9, ..., x_{n-2}, x_{n-1}, x_n]$
Full geometry Y $= [y_1, y_2, y_3, y_4, y_5, y_6, y_7, y_8, y_9, ..., y_{n-2}, y_{n-1}, y_n]$

(lv_1) $B_1 = [1, 0, 0, 1, 1, 0, 0, 1, 0, ..., 1, 0, 1]$
(lv_2) $B_2 = [1, 1, 0, 1, 1, 1, 0, 1, 0, ..., 1, 0, 1]$
(lv_3) $B_3 = [1, 1, 0, 1, 1, 1, 1, 1, 0, ..., 1, 1, 1]$

Fig. 4. Naive solution.

Figure 4 illustrates how this solution works for a geometry with three different levels of detail represented by the bitvectors B_1, B_2 and B_3. It should be noted that while there are two integer vectors corresponding to the X and Y axis, only one bitvector is necessary per level of detail. This is because a point with two coordinate values either appears or not at a specific level of detail, meaning that for any x_i its pair will share the same position on the Y axis vector.

Thanks to these bitvectors, we can implement the $res \leftarrow$ retrieve(ps, pe, lv_i) operation. Executing $succesor_1$ (detailed in Sect. 2.2) repeatedly over B_i from the position $ps - 1$ until reaching or surpassing the position pe returns all the positions on B_i set to 1, which are all the positions that describe the geographical object at the level of detail lv_i. We start at the position $ps - 1$ and not ps in order to also check whether $B_i[ps]$ is set to 1.

In Fig. 4, if a query demands the segment defined from x_3 ($ps = 3$) to x_8 ($pe = 8$) at the level of detail $lv_i = 2$; we would start by performing

$successor_1(B_2, 2) = 4$. Then, we calculate $succesor_1(B_2, 4) = 5$ and so on until reaching or surpassing $pe = 8$. Thus, in the example we get that the points that define the geometry segment between the points $ps = 3$ and $pe = 8$ at $lv = 2$ are $res = [(x_4, y_4), (x_5, y_5), (x_6, y_6), (x_8, y_8)]$. Note that for recovering the last level of detail we only need to return all the points stored as the full geometry of the object between positions ps and pe.

3.2   Proposal 2: Differential Solution

For our second approach, we propose an improved version of the *Naive Solution* using the inherent spatial locality of the data to reduce the size of the representation. As the first law of geography states, *everything is related to everything else, but near things are more related than distant things* [8]. In our particular context, this implies that points close to each other in a geometry representation would also have close coordinates (latitude and longitude). Therefore, the difference between two close-by values of such coordinates would be a significantly smaller value that could most likely be codified using a reduced amount of bits in opposition to the actual values of the real coordinates.

The first step to work with differential encoding is to sample each axis of the original geometry dividing them into two vectors: one storing some of the original values (absolutes), and another one containing relative values to those absolutes. A relative value is calculated using the positive difference between the original value and the closest previous absolute value. Essentially, for a point value x_i, its value in the relative values vector is equal to $|x_i - x_j|$, with $j = rank_1(B_1, i)$.

The original values would then be recovered by adding the corresponding absolute to the relative value. Two auxiliary bitvectors (one per axis) are needed to determine if the relative value results into a positive or a negative point. See Fig. 5 for clarification, although it should be noted that for simplicity sake the figure only illustrates the X axis.

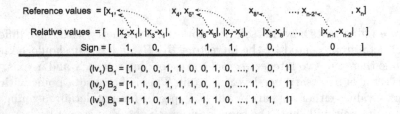

Fig. 5. Differential solution.

Observe how we use the points for the first level of detail $lv_i = 1$ as our absolute values. Given that it has the least amount of points, we consider it the most reasonable choice for reducing the storage space. Besides, using the points of an already defined level of detail lv_i means there is no need to define an additional bitvector for the absolute vectors (we use B_i). It also means that, if a query requests that particular level lv_i, we can simply return the absolute vectors with no further processing.

The operation $res \leftarrow \texttt{retrieve}(ps, pe, lv_i)$ is solved basically using the same algorithm as in our *Naive Solution* solution, except that this time it is necessary to consider if the value is an absolute value or a relative one, being mandatory to convert it accordingly to its original value in the second case.

3.3   Proposal 3: Binary-Naive Solution

The main idea behind this solution is that, for a low level of detail, it is not necessary to use values with much precision. For example, for the first level of detail (the least detailed representation of the geometry), it might be enough to use the b most significant bits of the actual integer values that might correspond to a precision adequate for representing the map at a high enough scale.

Again, this proposal is based on our *Naive Solution* but improving the data recovering working with bit-chunks depending on the level of detail lv_i instead of recovering the full values. As such, we called this our *Binary-Naive Solution*. Figure 6a illustrates how in this solution successive levels of detail do not add only new points, but they also add more precision to the points already included in the superior levels.

	x_1	x_2	x_3	x_{n-1}	x_n
Lv. 1 =	111	111	111	... 110	110
Lv. 2 =	11110	11110	11110	... 11011	11101
Lv. 3 =	10100	10100	10101	... 11101	01010
Lv. 4 =	01001	00110	00001	... 11001	10111

$(lv_1)\,B_1 = [1,\ 0,\ 0,\ 1,\ 1,\ 0,\ 0,\ 1,\ 0,\ ...,1,\ 0,\ 1]$
$(lv_2)\,B_2 = [1,\ 1,\ 0,\ 1,\ 1,\ 1,\ 0,\ 1,\ 0,\ ...,1,\ 0,\ 1]$
$(lv_3)\,B_3 = [1,\ 1,\ 0,\ 1,\ 1,\ 1,\ 1,\ 1,\ 0,\ ...,1,\ 1,\ 1]$

(a) Binary-Naive Solution.

	x_1	x_2	x_3	x_{n-1}	x_n	
Lv. 1 =	111	111	111	... 110	110	$XP_1 = [1,0,0,...,1,0]$
Lv. 2 =	11110	11110	11110	... 11011	11101	$XP_2 = [1,0,0,...,1,1]$
Lv. 3 =	10100	10100	10101	... 11101	01010	$XP_3 = [1,0,1,...,1,1]$
Lv. 4 =	01001	00110	00001	... 11001	10111	$XP_4 = [1,1,1,...,1,1]$

$(lv_1)\,B_1 = [1,\ 0,\ 0,\ 1,\ 1,\ 0,\ 0,\ 1,\ 0,\ ...,1,\ 0,\ 1]$
$(lv_2)\,B_2 = [1,\ 1,\ 0,\ 1,\ 1,\ 1,\ 0,\ 1,\ 0,\ ...,1,\ 0,\ 1]$
$(lv_3)\,B_3 = [1,\ 1,\ 0,\ 1,\ 1,\ 1,\ 1,\ 1,\ 0,\ ...,1,\ 1,\ 1]$

(b) Compressed-Chunks Solution.

Fig. 6. Our two binary solutions. *Binary-Naive* (left) just expands the coordinates through every level while *Compressed-Chunks* (right) also gets rid of repeated chunks.

For every level of detail lv_i, we need to define the length of the bit-chunk bl_i that corresponds to that level representation. Any distribution is possible, even assigning an unequal numbers of bits to the different levels. For our example in the Fig. 6a, we use 18 bit integers divided into 4 levels of detail. We assign 3 bits to the first level and 5 bits to the three next levels of detail.

The $res \leftarrow \texttt{retrieve}(ps, pe, lv)$ operation can be implemented mostly the same as before. The only difference is that instead of recovering the points that are included in the representation of a given level of detail lv_i, only the b most significant bits of the binary representation of that points are recovered, being b the total number of bits that would correspond to that level, plus the bit-chunks of any previous level. So, looking at the example in the Fig. 6a, for recovering x_3

at the level of detail 3 we would not return the value of x_3 but its 13 $(3+5+5)$ most representative bits, that is: 111 from the first level, 11110 from the second and 10100 from the third.

3.4   Proposal 4: Compressed-Chunks Solution

Our final proposal expands the *Binary-Naive Solution*. Given the same principle of spatial locality we took advantage from on our *Differential Solution*, we assume consecutive points would have fairly close-by numerical values, and therefore similar binary representations on the most significant bits. Therefore, the main idea behind this solution is to only store the bit-chunks on any given level that are different from the immediate previously stored bit-chunk. We call this approach our *Compressed-Chunks Solution*.

Figure 6b illustrates this solution. We have greyed out the bit-chunks that are not stored. Observe how the first 3 most significant bits that we would recover for the first level of detail of x_2 and x_3 are equal to those of x_1. Therefore, we do not need to store them. Instead, we will store a maximum of N bitvectors per axis of size n (n being the total number of points in the full geometry) where we set a 1 in the positions corresponding to a bit-chunk actually stored at that level of detail. These bitvectors are denoted as XP_1 to XP_4 in the Fig. 6b. Following the previous example, as we store the 3 most significant bits of x_1 at the level of detail lv_1, we set $XP_1[1]$ to 1, however, we leave $XP_1[2]$ and $XP_1[3]$ set to 0. Another N bitvectors would be necessary for the Y axis values.

Whereas it is fair to assume the 3 or even the 8 or 13 most significant bits of consecutive values would be equal (as Fig. 6b exemplifies with x_1 and x_2), no two points will ever be the same. It could be argued that it is inefficient to store the two bitvectors XP_N and YP_N corresponding to the last level of detail and the bit-chunks of least significant bits, as most if not all its positions would end up set to 1 like in the example for XP_4. Additionally, for this solution we need to process the two axis bitvectors XP_i and YP_i separately to recover the level of detail lv_i. Observe how, while in the Fig. 6b the 3 most significant bits of x_2 are equal to those of x_1 (stored as the first 3 bits bit-chunk for the first level of detail), it might be the case that the 3 most significant bits of y_2 are different from those of y_1, and therefore stored as a different 3 bit-chunk.

The operation $res \leftarrow \texttt{retrieve}(ps, pe, lv)$ functions mostly the same as in the *Binary-Naive Solution* with the exception that this time it is necessary to correctly select the bit-chunks corresponding to any value taking into account the information provided by XP_i and YP_i. Essentially, we use the $rank_1$ operation over the XP and YP vectors. For every position p we want to recover, its bit-chunk at any given level of detail i corresponds to the appropriated bit-chunk of the point at $rank_1(XP_i, p)$ and $rank_1(YP_i, p)$.

4   Experimental Evaluation

This section describes the experiments performed to test the efficiency of our proposals, comparing their space usage reduction and their query performance.

As a baseline, we filled a PostgreSQL database with the complete geometry outlining the border of the United States of America. The data was downloaded from the online repository GADM[1] as a collection of geographical points on decimal degrees that was then rounded to a precision of 4 decimal places as this would suffice to display the world with enough detail to display streets and buildings. From this geometry, three less detailed representations were computed applying the Douglas-Peucker [2] algorithm recursively. This resulted in four different representations of the border of the United States of America at four different levels of detail that amounted to a size of roughly 84 megabytes.

Table 1. Size usage of the four proposals (in Mb and in compression-ratio relative to the size of the original database)

Solution	Size (in Mb)	Compression-ratio (in %)
PostgreSQL database	84.39	100
Vector of 32-bit integers	42.19	50
Naive solution	10.36	12.28
Differential solution	8.62	10.22
Binary-Naive solution	10.36	12.28
Compressed-Chunks solution	**5.38**	**6.37**

Table 1 shows the sizes and compression ratios (defined as the percentage that the compressed representation occupies with respect to the original data) achieved by our proposals comparing against the PostgreSQL database. We also included the cost in megabytes of storing the four levels as 32-bit integer vectors. As expected, both the *Naive* and *Binary-Naive Solution* share the same compression-ratio. The *Differential Solution* demonstrates an improvement over both these solutions thanks to its smaller integer vectors, although, not as dramatic as the improvement shown by the the *Compressed-Chunks Solution*.

Table 2. Time comparison of all the solutions for recovering each full level of the cartographic generalization (in ms)

Level	Naive solution	Differential solution	Binary-Naive solution	Compressed-Chunks solution		
				Coordinate X	Coordinate Y	Total
1	84.385	**70.793**	83.318	60.045	61.855	121.900
2	**143.121**	198.343	145.144	181.291	188.364	369.655
3	**181.399**	270.279	186.166	314.196	313.736	627.932
4	**186.805**	291.396	187.212	405.504	406.804	812.308

Next, we study the query performance of each approach comparing the time each solution needed to retrieve the complete geometry of an object at each

[1] https://gadm.org/index.html.

level of detail, lv_1 to l_4. For the sake of fairness, we decided that every solution needed to return the same data type: a generic C vector of 32-bit integers. For every level of detail lv_i, we repeated the experiment 1,000 times and the times displayed in Table 2 are the mean value of those repetitions in milliseconds.

The *Naive Solution* is the fastest one for the second, third and fourth levels of detail, just surpassed by the *Differential Solution* when returning the first level. This happens because the first level in the *Differential Solution* are used as the sample points, which are stored separately and therefore can be recovered directly without need to access the corresponding bitvector, but its performance drops below both the *Naive* and the *Binary-Naive Solution* for every other level.

Finally, the *Compressed-Chunks Solution* demonstrates the worst performance for every level when taking into account the need to process the two axis separately. Additionally, even when accounting for only one axis, even if the *Compressed-Chunks Solution* starts obtaining better results than the alternatives on the first level, and better than the *Differential Solution* on the second, it is still the worst performing solution for the third and last levels.

Note that all of these experiments were run with the data structures already loaded into main memory. We would need to add the loading time of the data from disk to these processing times. This loading time would be comparable to a SELECT statement in PostgreSQL to retrieve a level of detail.

5   Conclusions and Future Work

As stated before, classic GIS solutions store several versions of the same cartographic objects to ease their management. Our work introduces four new representations that gather those advantages of classic approaches while using a unique representation for each cartographic object, i.e. our proposals can store the geometry of an object with variable granularity without storing several representations of it.

Despite being a work in progress, we have obtained promising results reducing the used space by state-of-the-art solutions more than a 85%. Our *Compressed-Chunks* approach improves that result achieving a 93% space footprint reduction.

As future work, the main aim would be to speed up the query times without worsening the space reductions achieved. This can be reached using compact data structures [5], which have self-indexing properties that enable fast access to the data.

References

1. Cotelo Lema, J.A., Barcon-Goas, M., Fariña, A., Luaces, M.R.: Combining geometry simplification and coordinate approximation techniques for better lossy compression of GIS data. In: Proceedings of DCC13, p. 482 (2013)
2. Douglas, D., Peucker, T.: Algorithms for the reduction of the number of points required to represent a digitized line or its caricature. Cartographica **10**(2), 112–122 (1973)

3. Gog, S., Beller, T., Moffat, A., Petri, M.: From theory to practice: plug and play with succinct data structures. In: Proceedings of SEA14, pp. 326–337 (2014)
4. Jacobson, G.J.: Succinct static data structures (1989)
5. Navarro, G.: Compact Data Structures: a practical approach (2016)
6. Ruas, A.: Map Generalization, pp. 631–632 (2008)
7. Shea, K.S., McMaster, R.B.: Cartographic generalization in a digital environment: when and how to generalize (1989)
8. Tobler, W.R.: A computer movie simulating urban growth in the detroit region. Econ. Geogr. 46(sup1), 234–240 (1970)

Towards Indoor Navigation Under Imprecision

Amina Hossain$^{(\boxtimes)}$, Matt Duckham, and Maria Vasardani

Department of Geospatial Science, RMIT University, Melbourne, VIC, Australia
amina.hossain@student.rmit.edu.au

Abstract. Indoor navigation systems help people to navigate through indoor environments. Conventional models of indoor navigation commonly assume that a navigator's location can be precisely determined. However, the limitations of indoor positioning systems as well as personal privacy constraints mean it is not always possible to determine individual's position precisely. This paper proposes an approach to developing new algorithms and tools for enabling indoor navigation under imprecision.

Keywords: Indoor navigation · Imprecision · Graph · Routing

1 Introduction

Applications for providing navigation assistance to wayfinders are at least as important in indoor environments as outdoors. A key part of indoor navigation assistance involves planning feasible routes through the indoor environment, and then guiding the user along the routes to reach the desired destination. Indoor navigation is especially important because arguably most navigation happens indoors, whether in shopping centres or airports, hospitals or universities, workplaces or leisure spaces. Recent studies indicate that people spend up to 87% of their time on average indoors [1–3], with likely at least some of that time spent wayfinding in unfamiliar indoor environments. Yet most navigation systems are designed primarily to support outdoor navigation. Therefore, building efficient wayfinding assistance for indoor navigators is an important research priority.

Indoor navigation under imprecision presents particular research challenges, when compared with outdoor navigation. Firstly, reliable and ubiquitous indoor positioning remains a significant challenge, as global navigation satellite systems (GNSS) cannot be easily used indoors [2]. Other indoor positioning techniques include radio frequency identification (RFID), infrared (IR), sensor networks, standard Wi-Fi positioning, and inertial navigation systems (dead reckoning). However, such approaches carry their own limitations, and are not nearly so well developed or ubiquitous as GNSS [4,5]. Recently, several studies have focused on the design and construction of positioning systems in GNSS-denied indoor environments [6]. Movement indoors is constrained by the architectural structures, such as doors, floors, corridors, and walls. While on the one hand, these

© Springer Nature Switzerland AG 2022
F. Karimipour and S. Storandt (Eds.): W2GIS 2022, LNCS 13238, pp. 82–92, 2022.
https://doi.org/10.1007/978-3-031-06245-2_8

constraints may help in providing meaningful location information at the logical and topological levels; on the other hand, the task of achieving accurate indoor localization is not straightforward [7].

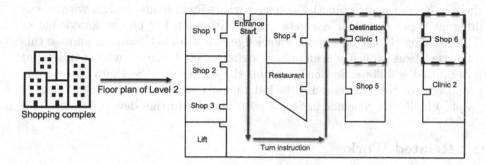

Fig. 1. An example scenario of a user's location privacy is being breached based in indoor environment.

Secondly, while established approaches to outdoor navigation, at city- and national-scale, are well investigated [8,10–13], these outdoor approaches typically assume a navigator's location can be precisely determined. Although all location sensing technology (both indoor and outdoor) is inherently imprecise, imprecision is a particular problem for indoor navigation. In addition to the challenges of indoor positioning, mentioned above, the level of precision required for accurate localization in indoor-scale environments can be much higher (where for example a meter or centimetres can be the difference between one side of a wall and the other) [9].

Thirdly, location privacy is a growing concern, as the number of smart, wearable, and IoT (Internet of Things) devices collecting location information continues to grow [33]. Personal location information is sensitive, with information such as home address, travel, and visits to locations such as medical clinics etc. among many examples of sensitive personal data [34]. More surprisingly, one study has indicated that four randomly chosen spatio-temporal points are enough to uniquely identify 95% of the individuals [35]. Indoor navigators may have reasonable expectations to be able to restrict the information they share about their precise location. Again, it is in the nature of indoor environments that these privacy concerns can be especially salient, and so sensitive. The difference of a few meters, even a few centimeters, can be the difference between a secure restricted area versus a public space, a hospital ward versus a waiting room, or a bar versus a gym. Such differences can have significant privacy implications, especially when considering unscrupulous companies or individuals. Consider the example scenario in Fig. 1, let us assume a navigator who regularly visits a medical clinic that is situated at level 2 inside a big shopping complex. This piece of information might be unfairly collected and used by unscrupulous shop owner from shop #6 in order to target the user for particular products or deny particular services.

Whether for privacy reasons, or the inherent imprecision of indoor positioning systems, this study aims to investigate the case or indoor navigation where an indoor navigator's actual location *cannot* be precisely determined. We propose an efficient approach designed to aid users in such a situation. We believe that there may exist many potential scenarios where an individual might wish access different types of indoor navigation aids without using precise knowledge of their location. To the best of our knowledge, our work is the first to address this important issue explicitly in an indoor environment. The remainder of this paper is organized as follows. Section 2 explains the background. Section 3 outlines our proposed structure, representing the indoor space as a connected, directed multi-graph. Finally, we conclude in Sect. 4 with plan for further developments.

2   Related Work

In this section, we review some of the existing literature that bears on our contribution. The relevant literature falls into two main areas of relevance: representations of indoor environments and algorithms for generating navigation instructions, including navigation instructions under imprecision.

2.1   Representing Indoor Environments

Indoor environments contain different types of enclosed spaces, such as rooms and corridors, each with their own affordances and functions. When modeling indoor spaces, one of the most natural and effective representations for navigation is as a graph. The influential work of [16] on space syntax investigates the interior of a building and its relation to social properties. In space syntax, cells or subdivisions of a cell are represented as points while doors or entrances are represented as links (i.e., edges) between two points. All corridors that are interconnected directly are aggregated into one node, not always appropriate for complex and large corridors.

The topology of graph-based indoor models sometimes also uses geometry in its construction. Intervisibility, for example, has been used to construct indoor graphs where edges connect nodes that are mutually intervisible along the line-of-sight [17,18]. However, this approach can lead to a proliferation of unnecessary or duplicative edge connections in the resulting graph [15]. An alternative graph based indoor model uses the *straight skeleton* from computational geometry, constructing the network from the polygonal floor layout [19–21]. Lee [19] developed a straight medial axis transformation algorithm (S-MAT) to create this network from the floor geometry. For simple and relatively regular polygons, straight skeleton based methods such as S-MAT can generate good results. However, in some complex cases, they too can produce many superfluous nodes and edges, unnecessary for human wayfinding [14].

Addressing these issues, Clementini and Pagliaro [22] proposed automated indoor network generation method by eliminating routes that were deemed unnatural for humans to follow (i.e., a path or paths with narrow angles, too close to walls and obstacles). In this model, a straight skeleton of the floor map is filtered using edge length and intervisibility criteria. We adopt this model in our work to represent our indoor environments.

2.2 Generating Navigation Instructions

Several alternative approaches to routing outdoors have been developed, such as shortest paths, the fewest turns [23] and the simplest instructions [10]. These algorithms can be well utilised in the outdoor routing. Most solutions fundamentally vary the costs associated with edges or nodes in the graph, and use the Dijkstra algorithm [25] to minimize the cost through the graph from origin to destination.

Indoor environments arguably differ from outdoor environments in the wider diversity of types of indoor spaces, from museums, convention halls, and airports to office buildings, hotels, and apartment complexes. Hence, outdoor routing approaches are not always well-suited to indoor routing applications [24]. Consequently, several attempts have been made by indoor navigation researchers to improve the route calculations for indoor environments. A simple solution was proposed by Khan et al. [26] by optimizing travel time based on estimated speeds, differentiating between regular walked segments and stairs. In related research on evacuation, the focus of path planning is on speed, but risk, population density, accessibility, user restrictions, and turns are also considered [27].

Clementini and D'Orazio [28] proposed a routing instructions algorithm for indoor navigators that guides them to reach a desired destination within a typical building floor. The approach uses the graph-based representation of Clementini and Pagliaro [22] introduced above. The approach works effectively in terms of guiding indoor visitors to reach their destination, but does not consider the issues arising from imprecision of location. Hence, this work focuses on bridging the gap between such indoor navigation system, and the inherent imprecision of indoor positions.

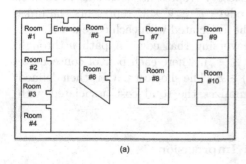
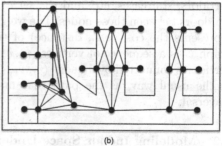

(a)   (b)

Fig. 2. Case study floor plan (a) and resulting navigation network for the case study floor plan after adopting method from [22] (b)

Although most studies on human navigation deals exclusively with navigation where an agent's location can be precisely determined, some work has also begun to address the more general problem of navigation under imprecision. Chown [29] first examined the role of uncertainty in the PLAN model. Later, Raubal and Worboys [30] used rough sets to model imprecise knowledge in the navigation process. However, neither of these approaches addresses the issue of delivering location-based navigation services to an agent under imprecision. Duckham et al. in [9] does consider this issue directly, however. The approach aims to support outdoor navigation instruction generation when an individual's precise location is unknown. Acknowledging the special constraints and characteristics of indoor environments, this research extends such past work by explicitly addressing the issue of effective navigation under imprecision in indoor environments.

3   Methodology

In this section, we at first review the construction of the graph-based representation of an indoor space that supports imprecise navigation. Then we present the method for computing navigation instructions that help the navigator to navigate through an indoor space under imprecision.

3.1   Modelling Indoor Space

As indicated above, in this work we adopt an adaptation of the graph-based approach of [22] for representation of indoor environments (see Fig. 2).

We use a weighted, directed multigraph for modeling the indoor space. A multigraph is a graph where multiple distinct edges may exist between a pair of nodes; in contrast a regular graph may have at most one edge between any pair of nodes. A multigraph is important since at allows us to represent spaces where multiple different doors or access points may be available to move between two rooms. However, for simplicity let us assume here a simple weighted, directed graph $G = (V, E)$, where the set of vertices V represents locations in rooms, corridors, staircases, etc. and the set of edges $E \subseteq V \times V$ represents the links via doors between those nodes. The weight associated with each edge $w : E \to \mathbb{Z}$ represents the cost (e.g., distance) of traversing that edge. A path p through graph G is a sequence of vertices $(v_0, v_1, ..., v_n)$, where each pair of consecutive vertices is connected by an edge $(v_i, v_{i+1}) \in E$. The shortest path is then defined in the usual way, as the path that minimizes the total cost associated with traversal.

3.2   Modeling Indoor Space Under Imprecision

We adopt the model of imprecision proposed by Duckham et al. [9] into our indoor graph network, due to its simplicity. Imprecision refers to the lack of detail in information. There are two primary aspects to that lack of detail particularly relevant to indoor navigation.

First, there is a lack of detail in an individual's location information, either because the person is protecting their privacy or more often simply because we can not know their exactly position due to the precision limitations of indoor positioning systems. For example, let us assume that we do not know whether the person is in Room #1 or Room #2 and he/ she wants to navigate Room #7 (see Fig. 3(a)). Consider the instruction sequence: "leave the room; turn right; go to the end of the corridor; take the next left and the following left; and enter the second room on the right". Even though we do not know whether the person is in Room #1 or Room #2, this instruction sequence is expected to work well regardless of the lack of precision in origin location.

Second, there is also inherent imprecision in the turn instruction that we give people. For example, in Fig. 3(b), there are two distinct navigation paths with different origins and destinations (orange and red colour arrows) each described using the same turn instructions. Hence, in this work we aim to use this inherent imprecision of navigation instructions. Our work builds on this intuition that it should still be possible—in some cases at least—to navigate in indoor environments even under imprecision.

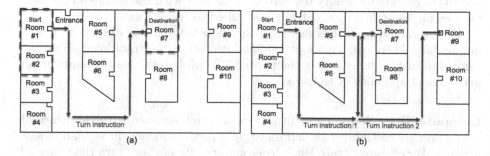

Fig. 3. Imprecision of a user location (a) and turn instructions (b) indoor.

More formally, we represent imprecision in location using an equivalence relation $\sim$ on the set of vertices V within our graph. Two vertices v_1, v_2 are related, $v_1 \sim v_2$, if they cannot be discerned apart by our positioning system, due to imprecision [9]. This indiscernibility relation $\sim$ is thus assumed to be reflexive ($v \sim v$), symmetric ($v_1 \sim v_2$ implies $v_2 \sim v_1$), and transitive ($v_1 \sim v_2$ and $v_2 \sim v_3$ implies $v_1 \sim v_3$). Therefore, our indiscernibility relation $\sim$ is defined as follows.

Definition 1 (Indiscernibility relation $\sim$). *An indiscernibility relation is an equivalence relationship on a set of vertices V within a graph G. That is reflexive ($v \sim v$), symmetric (if $v_1 \sim v_2$ then $v_2 \sim v_1$), and transitive (if $v_1 \sim v_2$ and $v_2 \sim v_3$ then $v_1 \sim v_3$) for any $v, v_1, v_2, v_3 \in V$.*

The set of locations indiscernible from a location $v \in V$ is the equivalence class of v, written $[v]$, where $[v] \in V/\sim$ ($V/\sim$ is called the *quotient set*, a partition of V). A navigator cannot directly use paths in the graph G for navigation under imprecision, since they refer to precise locations within the graph. Instead, the problem addressed is to create instructions suitable to follow a precise path in the graph, but with only imprecise knowledge of locations in that graph.

3.3 Generating Turn Sequences

In this section, we discuss how to generate turn sequences for our indoor environment. Generating turn sequences within an indoor environment is a required step in our proposed work. We first describe how to compute a shortest path for a given source and destination within our indoor graph and then demonstrate how to estimate turn sequences of the shortest path for a navigator. Then we explain all the possible steps of the turn sequences estimation algorithm in detail.

Compute Shortest Path. Dijkstra's algorithm [25] is the foundation of most shortest path algorithms. Dijkstra's algorithm maintains a set S of vertices whose final shortest path weights from the source s has already been determined. The algorithm repeatedly selects the vertex $u \in V - S$ with the minimum shortest path estimate, adds u to s and "relaxes" all edges leaving u.

However, standard Dijkstra's algorithm is not applicable directly to multi-graphs [31]. Therefore, we adopt modified version of the traditional Dijkstra's algorithm (detail discussion in the paper [32]), while retaining the same broad and efficient approach of Dijkstra.

Compute Turn Sequences. In general, a turn sequence is the sequence of navigation instructions to be performed by a person moving through an indoor network. For example, "turn left," "continue straight on," or "turn right" are all examples of navigation instructions. According to [10], instructions are typically considered at decision points where path alternatives are available.

We define a labeling function $f : V \times V \times V \rightarrow C$ for vertices $v \in V$ in a shortest path $p = (v_0, v_1, ..., v_n)$ using instruction label set C (e.g., $C = \{$turn left, turn right, ...$\}$). The instructions themselves are formed by examining the two directed, incident edges in the graph $(v_{i-1}, v_i) \in E$ and $(v_i, v_{i+1}) \in E$, in the context of the other edges in G incident with v_i. A four way intersection, for example, where (v_{i-1}, v_i), (v_i, v_{i+1}) form an approximate 90° counterclockwise angle will lead to node v_i being labeled with instruction "turn left" in the path p (i.e., $f(v_{i-1}, v_i, v_{i+1}) =$ turn left).

Using the labeling function, a sequence of instructions for following a path can be generated without directly referring to (precise) locations. For example, there is a path, $p = (v_0, v_1, ..., v_n)$ and labeling function f, the instruction sequence $I = (f(v_0, v_1, v_2), f(v_1, v_2, v_3), ...)$ needs to be generated. Note that the length of the instruction sequence is necessarily the length of the path minus 2.

Of course, an individual instruction may appear in more than one path, and indeed multiple times in a single path.

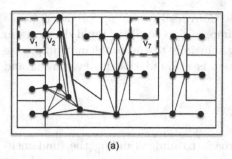 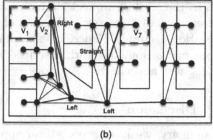

(a)   (b)

Fig. 4. Shortest path computation between source and destination (a) and turn instructions generation for the shortest path (b)

Follow Turn Instructions. Finally, to evaluate the turn sequences generated, we propose to use agent-based simulation. Simulation will enable rapid and scalable investigation of how agents could follow turn instructions under imprecision.

Take Fig. 4 as an example. Let us assume that an agent wants to navigate from somewhere in room 1 (imprecise location, equivalence class $\{v_1, v_2\} \in V/\sim$) to a precise a destination in room 7 (v_7, see Fig. 4(a)). The proposed algorithm arbitrarily selects any node from the equivalence class $\{v_1, v_2\}$ as a start node (let us assume that v_2 is selected arbitrarily as a start node from the equivalence class $\{v_1, v_2\}$). Then it computes the shortest path from the selected node v_2 to the destination v_7, generating the turn instruction for that shortest path (see Fig. 4(b)).

Then the algorithm executes the sequence of turn instructions, making the agent follow each instruction in turn while ignoring any instructions that cannot be completed. The algorithm terminates if it finds that the current location is in the equivalence class of the destination location $[v_7]$ (in this case the singleton, precise destination of v_7 alone), i.e., the agent has reached its destination successfully.

3.4 Development and Evaluation

From this basis, the effectiveness of different extensions and variations to our algorithm can be evaluated by measuring the navigation accuracy, for example, in terms of the success rates of simulated navigation agents in reaching their destination. In brief, the proposed algorithm performance will be evaluated by comparing the level of imprecision with navigation accuracy. The level of imprecision refers how precisely we have located. For example, high levels of imprecision mean we have little information about where exactly the person is located; low levels of imprecision mean that we know precisely the person's location. Navigation accuracy refers how close to the destination the user gets using the generated instruction sequences. There are two extremes of outcomes from the algorithm performance evaluation. Ideally, good performance means that the algorithm will continue to provide high levels of navigation accuracy even as the level of imprecision increases. Conversely, poor performance means that even small increases in the level of imprecision result in rapid decreases in navigation accuracy. Hence, in exploring solutions to the problem of imprecise indoor navigation, the work described here is a foundation for evaluating and refining new and effective solutions.

3.5 Discussion

In summary, we have proposed an approach to understanding the fundamentals of what we can compute under imprecision indoors. In our approach, an indoor environment is represented as a graph and imprecision in location is represented as an equivalence relation, with equivalence classes giving the "grains" of indiscernible node sets within the graph. The algorithm presented in this work provides a way to generate navigation instructions not simply from nodes, as is usual in shortest paths, but from sets of nodes (i.e., indiscernible equivalence classes of nodes). In this way, we aim to guide an navigator to his or her desired destination under this framework, even when precise location is unknown.

Several key issues not covered in this paper will need to be addressed and these include: richer and more sophisticated indoor representations; richer and more sophisticated instruction sets, for example incorporating a wider range of possible instructions or references to environmental signs or landmarks; and more sophisticated imprecise navigation algorithms, such as including incremental instructions based on (imprecise) location tracking; using learning approaches to improve performance over time, or in response to navigation errors; or assuming imprecise destination as well as imprecise navigator location.

4 Conclusion

This working paper focuses on understanding the fundamentals of what navigation instructions it is possible to compute under imprecision indoors. Imprecision refers to the lack of detail in information. Our approach aims to discover the best ways to create useful indoor navigation services utilising this limited information. We are progressing towards the completion of the proposed algorithm's implementation based on the proposed data structure, as the preliminary step to extensive simulation, validation, and evaluation.

References

1. Dörre, W.H.: Time-activity-patterns of some selected small groups as a basis for exposure estimation: a methodological study. J. Expo. Anal. Environ. Epidemiol. **7**(4), 471–491 (1981)
2. Worboys, M.: Modeling indoor space. In: Proceedings of the 3rd ACM SIGSPATIAL International Workshop on Indoor Spatial Awareness, pp. 1–6 (2011)
3. Jensen, C.S., Li, K.J., Winter, S.: ISA 2010 workshop report: the other 87%: a report on the second international workshop on indoor spatial awareness (San Jose, California-November 2, 2010). SIGSPATIAL Spec. **3**(1), 10–12 (2011)

4. Yang, L., Worboys, M.: Similarities and differences between outdoor and indoor space from the perspective of navigation. Poster presented at COSIT (2011)
5. Correa, A., Barcelo, M., Morell, A. and Vicario, J.L.: A review of pedestrian indoor positioning systems for mass market applications. Sensors **17**(8), 1927 (2017). 181–184. IEEE Press, New York (2001)
6. Kolodziej, K.W., Hjelm, J.: Local Positioning Systems: LBS Applications and Services. CRC Press, Boca Raton (2017)
7. Afyouni, I., Ray, C., Christophe, C.: Spatial models for context-aware indoor navigation systems: a survey. J. Spat. Inf. Sci. **1**(4), 85–123 (2012)
8. Raubal, M., Winter, S.: Enriching wayfinding instructions with local landmarks. In: Egenhofer, M.J., Mark, D.M. (eds.) GIScience 2002. LNCS, vol. 2478, pp. 243–259. Springer, Heidelberg (2002). https://doi.org/10.1007/3-540-45799-2_17
9. Duckham, M., Kulik, L., Worboys, M.: Imprecise navigation. GeoInformatica **7**(2), 79–94 (2003)
10. Duckham, M., Kulik, L.: "Simplest" paths: automated route selection for navigation. In: Kuhn, W., Worboys, M.F., Timpf, S. (eds.) COSIT 2003. LNCS, vol. 2825, pp. 169–185. Springer, Heidelberg (2003). https://doi.org/10.1007/978-3-540-39923-0_12
11. Haque, S., Kulik, L., Klippel, A.: Algorithms for reliable navigation and wayfinding. In: Barkowsky, T., Knauff, M., Ligozat, G., Montello, D.R. (eds.) Spatial Cognition 2006. LNCS (LNAI), vol. 4387, pp. 308–326. Springer, Heidelberg (2007). https://doi.org/10.1007/978-3-540-75666-8_18
12. Cuayáhuitl, H., Dethlefs, N., Frommberger, L., Richter, K.-F., Bateman, J.: Generating adaptive route instructions using hierarchical reinforcement learning. In: Hölscher, C., Shipley, T.F., Olivetti Belardinelli, M., Bateman, J.A., Newcombe, N.S. (eds.) Spatial Cognition 2010. LNCS (LNAI), vol. 6222, pp. 319–334. Springer, Heidelberg (2010). https://doi.org/10.1007/978-3-642-14749-4_27
13. Amores, D., Tanin, E., Vasardani, M.: A proactive route planning approach to navigation errors. Int. J. Geogr. Inf. Sci. **35**(6), 1094–1130 (2021)
14. Yang, L., Worboys, M.: Generation of navigation graphs for indoor space. Int. J. Geogr. Inf. Sci. **29**(10), 1737–1756 (2015)
15. Liu, L. and Zlatanova, S.: Simplest instructions: Finding easy-to-describe routes for navigation. a "door-to-door" path-finding approach for indoor navigation. In: Proceedings Gi4DM 2011: Geo Information for Disaster Management, Antalya, Turkey, 3–8 May 2011
16. Hillier, B., Hanson, J.: The Social Logic of Space. Cambridge University Press, Cambridge (1989)
17. Franz, G., Wiener, J.M.: From space syntax to space semantics: a behaviorally and perceptually oriented methodology for the efficient description of the geometry and topology of environments. Environ. Plan. b: Plan. Des. **35**(4), 574–592 (2008)
18. Kneidl, A., Borrmann, A., Hartmann, D.: Generation and use of sparse navigation graphs for microscopic pedestrian simulation models. Adv. Eng. Inf. **26**(4), 669–680 (2012)
19. Lee, J.: A spatial access-oriented implementation of a 3-D GIS topological data model for urban entities. GeoInformatica **8**(3), 237–264 (2004)
20. Lee, J.: Simplest instructions: Finding easy-to-describe routes for navigation. A three-dimensional navigable data model to support emergency response in microspatial built-environments. Ann. Assoc. Am. Geogr. **97**(3), 512–529 (2007)
21. Worboys, M.F., Duckham, M.: GIS: a Computing Perspective. CRC Press, Boca Raton (2004)

22. Clementini, E., Pagliaro, A.: The construction of a network for indoor navigation. In: GISTAM, pp. 254–261 (2020)

23. Hillier, B., Iida, S.: Network effects and psychological effects: a theory of urban movement. In: Proceedings of the 5th International Symposium on Space Syntax, vol. 1, pp. 553–564, Delft: TU Delft (2005)

24. Chow, J.C., Peter, M., Scaioni, M., Al-Durgham, M.: Indoor tracking, mapping, and navigation: algorithms, technologies, and applications (2018)

25. Dijkstra, E.W.: A note on two problems in connexion with graphs. Numerische mathematik 1(1), 269–271 (1959)

26. Khan, A.A., Yao, Z., Kolbe, T.H.: Simplest instructions: finding easy-to-describe routes for navigation. Context aware indoor route planning using semantic 3D building models with cloud computing. In: Breunig, M., Al-Doori, M., Butwilowski, E., Kuper, P., Benner, J., Haefele, K. (eds.) 3D Geoinformation Science, pp. 175–192, Springer, Cham (2015). https://doi.org/10.1007/978-3-319-12181-9_11

27. Wang, J., Zhao, H., Winter, S.: Integrating sensing, routing and timing for indoor evacuation. Fire Saf. J. 78, 111–121 (2015)

28. Clementini, E., D'Orazio, V.: Qualitative routing instructions in indoor space. ISPRS Ann. Photogrammetry Remote Sens. Spat. Inf. Sci. 6, 47–53 (2020)

29. Chown, E.: Making predictions in an uncertain world: Environmental structure and cognitive maps. Adapt. Behav. 7(1), 17–33 (1999)

30. Raubal, M., Worboys, M.: A formal model of the process of wayfinding in built environments. In: Freksa, C., Mark, D.M. (eds.) COSIT 1999. LNCS, vol. 1661, pp. 381–399. Springer, Heidelberg (1999). https://doi.org/10.1007/3-540-48384-5_25

31. Cormen, T.H., Leiserson, C.E., Rivest, R.L., Stein, C.: Introduction to Algorithms. MIT Press, Cambridge (2009)

32. Biswas, S.S., Alam, B., Doja, M.N.: Generalization of Dijkstra's algorithm for extraction of shortest paths in directed multigraphs. J. Comput. Sci. 9(3), 377–382 (2013)

33. Perez, A.J., Zeadally, S.: Privacy issues and solutions for consumer wearables. IT Prof. 20(4), 46–56 (2018)

34. Duckham, M., Kulik, L.: Location privacy and location-aware computing. In: Dynamic and Mobile GIS, pp. 377–382. CRC Press, Boca Raton (2006)

35. De Montjoye, Y.A., Hidalgo, C.A., Verleysen, M.: Unique in the crowd: the privacy bounds of human mobility. Sci. Rep. 3, 1–5 (2013)

Bus Passenger Load Prediction: Challenges from an Industrial Experience

Flora Amato[1], Sergio Di Martino[1], Nicola Mazzocca[1], Davide Nardone[2],
Franca Rocco di Torrepadula[1(✉)], and Paolo Sannino[2]

[1] University of Naples Federico II, DIETI, via Claudio 21, 80125 Naples, Italy
{flora.amato,sergio.dimartino,nicola.mazzocca,
franca.roccoditorrepadula}@unina.it
[2] Hitachi Rail, via Argine 425, 80147 Naples, Italy
{davide.nardone,paolo.sannino}@hitachirail.com

Abstract. In times of ongoing pandemic outbreak, public transportation systems organisation and operation have been significantly affected. Among others, the necessity to implement in-vehicle social distancing has fostered new requirements, such as the possibility to know in advance how many people will likely be on a public bus at a given stop. This is very relevant for both potential passengers waiting at a stop, and for decision makers of a transit company, willing to adapt the operational planning. Within the domain of data-driven Intelligent Transportation Systems (ITS), some research activities are being conducted towards Bus Passenger Load (BPL) predictions, with contrasting results. In this paper we report on an academic/industrial experience we conducted to predict BPL in a major Italian city, using real-world data. In particular, we describe the difficulties and challenges we had to face in the data processing and mining steps, due to multiple data sources, with noisy data. As a consequence, in this paper we highlight to the ITS community the need of more advanced techniques and approaches suitable to support the instantiation of a data analytic pipeline for BPL prediction.

Keywords: Bus passenger load prediction · Smart mobility · Pandemic · Geosensor data · Telematics

1 Introduction

In the last years, also due to the rapid demographic growth of cities, it is pretty common that transportation systems are struggling to satisfy the needs of urban mobility, with the demand of commuters being often higher than the transport supply [1–4]. This leads, among other, to in-vehicle crowding, which is cause of stress, anxiety and loss of productivity for passengers, while also increasing dwell and waiting times [5–7].

Within the ITS domain, a lot of research efforts have been aimed at improving urban public transportation systems. For example, many works have addressed the problem of predicting metro or bus arrival times (*e.g.* [8–10]). More recently,

© Springer Nature Switzerland AG 2022
F. Karimipour and S. Storandt (Eds.): W2GIS 2022, LNCS 13238, pp. 93–107, 2022.
https://doi.org/10.1007/978-3-031-06245-2_9

some researches aimed at defining novel techniques and solutions to predict in vehicle crowding (*e.g.* [11,12]). This research area, known as *Bus Passenger Load (BPL) Prediction*, aims at forecasting how many people will be present on buses, using historical crowding data (*e.g.* [11]) and/or models, such as Original-Destination (OD) matrices (*e.g.* [13]). The key benefits of a BPL-based service are:

- Transport companies can better manage their own resources (*e.g.* vehicles and staff), in order to meet users' needs [13].
- Passengers can know how crowded the buses are. In this way they can plan their trip based on that information [14].
- Travel quality can be improved [14] and, as a result, it can promote the use of public transport rather than private one.

Last but not least, studies on BPL have been significantly fostered in times of ongoing pandemic outbreak. Indeed, during the COVID-19 pandemic, the concern that public transit poses a high risk of infectious disease transmission was prevalent [15,16]. For this reason, promoting *social distancing* was one of the key public health recommendations [15,17], but this makes it even more difficult for public transport to meet the commuters demands. Tirachini and Cats outline a broad range of measures to apply social distancing in public transportation, including rail and bus crowding management [18]. Thus, BPL predictive systems could be employed to implement social distancing, in order to keep vehicle occupancy rates under a predefined threshold [19,20].

Despite the many advantages provided by BPL predictions, it is recognised that there are still a number of open issues [7], compared to the relevant literature for rail transport crowding predictions (*e.g.* [21–25]). The problem seems to be more difficult to solve, compared to rail systems, also because data collection is more challenging, and affected by multiple external factors undermining data quality [7].

In this paper we report on an academic/industrial experience aimed at defining a BPL prediction system for a major Italian urban area. In particular, since March 2021, more than two dozens of buses were equipped with specific sensors to measure on-board crowding information, shared with a central back-end. There, some data preprocessing and mining techniques were defined to predict, for each route/stop of the urban area, the crowding of the next three buses passing by at the given stop of the given route.

The implementation of this system was far from trivial, with a number of difficulties, related to the context of spatio-temporal data management. In this paper, we describe the major challenges we faced and some of the strategies we applied to overcome them. Moreover, for each spatio-temporal data preprocessing/mining step, we highlight some topics that the research community on Geographical Information Systems could face, in order to ease the development of these types of systems for the intended ICT practitioners.

2   State of the Art on BPL Predictions

Within the ITS domain, some works have focused on defining novel techniques and solutions to predict Bus Passenger Load (BPL) (*e.g.* [11,12]). The general goal of BPL-related studies is to forecast the demand for bus use. This, one hand, can enable for better route planning and scheduling, while, on the other hand, can improve commuter's experience [26]. Let us note that the problem faced by BPL solutions is somehow similar to the relevant literature for rail transport crowding predictions (*e.g.* [21–25]), even if it is recognised that the number of researches carried out on predicting bus crowding is still limited [7], mainly due to the following problems:

1. The access to rail transportation systems is somehow more controlled than the buses. Thus, it is relatively easier to collect passenger load information regarding rail systems rather than buses.
2. Actual systems to determine the number of bus passengers are less reliable, giving rise to more noisy datasets.
3. Bus services can be disrupted by road traffic conditions, making the problem harder than the one regarding rail systems.

Some BPL-related studies address the problem as a (multi-class) classification one, where the goal is to predict a *level* of bus crowding. For example, Arabghalizi *et al.* [26] propose a method for BPL prediction, where the goal is to forecast the level of in-vehicle crowding. In particular, they forecast the passenger flow using a random forest, comparing 9 different types of potential features. The proposed approach require to train one model for each pair route-stop, leading to potentially significant scalability issues on a wider urban area. Similarly, Zuo *et al.* [27] propose the use of a Radial Basis Function Neural Network (RBFNN) to determine the future degree of bus crowding among six possible levels, namely: *very comfortable, comfortable, generally crowded, crowded, very crowded* and *unbearable*. The proposal has been preliminary evaluated using a dataset of the Chinese town of Dalian.

Other researchers set the problem as a regression one. For example, Wang *et al.* [7] suggest a two-step approach to predict the number of passenger on board. In a first step, the passenger flow for next stops is predicted, using a Kalman filter; in the second one, Support Vector Regression (SVR) is used for predicting the BPL. Jenelius propose and compare the use of LASSO regularized and multivariate partial least squares regressions to predict BPL. In a first study, he applied the proposed techniques on a dataset collected from buses from the city of Stockholm [11]. Then, he applied these techniques also on a dataset from a rail line, again collected in Stockholm [25]. The results show that the prediction accuracy for bus system is far behind the one for trains. As observed also by Wang *et al.*, this can be an indicator that predicting passenger loads on buses is more challenging than in a rail system [7].

Fig. 1. First type of crowding detection sensors.

3   The Investigated BPL Prediction Scenario

Within a collaboration between industrial and academic partners, we aimed at setting up a BPL prediction solution for a major Italian city, to face bus passenger limitations inducted by the pandemic restrictions. Since March 2021, about two dozens of buses were selected to be equipped with sensors able to count on-board passengers. The first problem to face was how to choose the type of sensors. There are many possible strategies to collect passenger load data, including Automated Fare Collection (AFC) systems, Automatic Passenger Counter (APC) systems, vehicle weight sensors, video recording data, sniffing of mobile/wireless networks (*e.g.* Bluetooth and Wi-Fi) or crowd-sourcing data (*e.g.* explicit user feedback in travel app) [13,28,29]. In our case, we opted for sensors based on processing videos acquired by specifically installed cameras. We employed sensing solutions provided by two different companies, installed on different buses, which operate in pretty different ways. The first one is based on multiple cameras installed on top of the vehicle doors, thus monitoring how many people get on and off the bus (see Fig. 1). The overall number of people on board is calculated from these information. The acquisition is triggered by an event system, every time a door opens, separately for each door. This system generates a dataset where each tuple corresponds to a door opening event. Each record is thus characterised by information on the number of boarding and alighting passengers, along with a timestamp and positioning data.

On the other hand, the second type of sensors collects directly in-vehicle occupancy, exploiting a single camera able to cover the interior of the bus (see Fig. 2).

This second system generates data in a different fashion. After an off-line processing, an *Occupancy* file is generated, with a tuple for each bus stop, containing directly the number of In-Vehicle passengers and a timestamp. Furthermore, a different *Location* file is generated, with a positioning information added every 30 s.

Given the data collected from buses, the goal of the project is to perform a BPL prediction for each pair route-stop. In particular, for a given route r, stop s, and time t, we aim at predicting the BPL of subsequent ho buses passing at the same route-stop rs, where the parameter ho is the *horizon*. To this aim, we

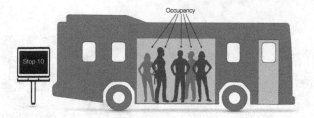

Fig. 2. Second type of crowding detection sensors.

want to exploit historical data collected from the last hi buses of the route r over the stop s, where hi is the number of considered *history* samples, to build the prediction model.

3.1 The Adopted Knowledge Discovery Process

The methodology we adopted to implement the project can be traced back to the Knowledge Discovery in Databases (KDD) process, which was firstly formalized by Fayyad et al. in [30] as the application "*of methods and techniques for making sense of data*". It consists of the following five key steps:

1. **Data Selection**, dealing with selecting a subset of data samples or variables on which discovery is to be performed.
2. **Preprocessing**, consisting in preprocessing the selected data, *e.g.* by defining ways to manage noise or missing information, and to normalise data.
3. **Transformation**, involving data reduction/projection in order to make the data as suitable as possible for the next data mining phase.
4. **Data Mining**, dealing with searching for unknown patterns in the considered data, typically using Artificial Intelligence (AI) techniques.
5. **Interpretation/Evaluation**, during which the identified patterns are submitted to a decision maker for interpretation, often using data visualisation techniques.

Let us note that the KDD process is not necessarily linear and may generally involve a significant iteration, with possible loops between any two steps [30].

A solution for BPL prediction can be seen as a particular instantiation of the KDD process.

3.2 An Architecture for BPL Prediction Systems

The reference architecture for our BPL prediction system is shown in Fig. 3 and consists of three different modules:

– The *Sensing* module involves the BPL acquisition system, through which both the crowding and position data are collected, plus the telemetry solution to send data to the remote back-end;

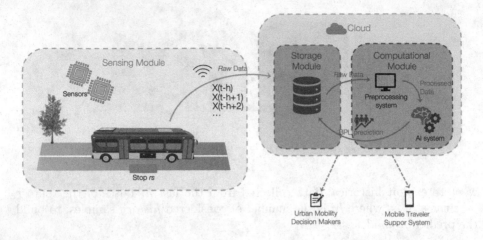

Fig. 3. Architecture of the developed BPL prediction system.

- The acquired data are memorised in the *Storage module*. In our implementation, it is deployed in a Cloud infrastructure, leveraging a solution based on PostGres-PostGIS.
- At the *Computational module* all the elaborations on the data are performed, from the preprocessing up to the actual predictions. This module is also deployed in a Cloud-based infrastructure.

In the following sections, we detail the challenges we faced in the implementation of this architecture.

4 The Preprocessing Phase: Challenges and Experiences

In this type of problems, the preprocessing phase is particularly complex and costly, due to the spatio-temporal nature of both the problem and the data. We start by describing the difficulties we encountered in this phase, highlighting also potential research directions.

Integration of Different Data Sources. To train a BPL prediction model, the example dataset should contain at least the following features:

- *Timestamp.* Store the entry timestamp.
- *Latitude/Longitude.* Indicate the coordinates of the vehicle.
- *Occupancy.* Contains the number of persons on board the vehicle

The key problem is that different acquisition systems may generate data with different formats. In our case, as detailed in Sect. 3, we have buses equipped with two different acquisition systems, each one collecting data in a distinct format. Indeed, the one generated by the system described in Fig. 1 does not explicitly contain the occupancy feature, as it is derived from two different attributes, i.e. the number of people entering and exiting each door d at time t ($on_{t,d}$ and $off_{t,d}$) features, in the following), calculated through the formula:

$$occupancy_t = occupancy_{t-1} + \sum_{d \in D} on_{t,d} - \sum_{d \in D} off_{t,d} \qquad (1)$$

On the other hand, the dataset generated by the acquisition system described in Fig. 2 consists of two different files, one related to the occupancy O, with a new record for each stop of the bus, and the other one related to the positioning P, with a new record every 30 s. Therefore, we need to associate each record of O to a record stored in P. To solve this issue we developed an algorithm matching each tuple in O to the one with the closest timestamp in P. Furthermore, we included some heuristics to consider plausibility of the sensor readings.

In our experience, just this preliminary integration phase of the two different datasets required over a month of coding/testing. A key benefit from the research community could be the definition of a standard data format for the occupancy data acquisition.

As a result of the previous step, every occupancy data is associated to a couple of latitude and longitude coordinates. Now, we need to align this information to the bus stops, whose coordinates are usually available in the General Transit Feed Specification (GTFS) format. This process is detailed in the next section.

Bus Stop Matching. To perform a BPL prediction, we need to clearly obtain bus crowding information, for each considered stop of a given route. As the bus positioning systems can be characterised by low-precision, we need to align Global Navigation Satellite System (GNSS) data with the correct geographical coordinates of the stops on a line. It is worth to point out that this type of alignment is different from traditional map-matching, mostly applied to trajectories (e.g.: [31]). Indeed, rather than requiring to align a series of position points to a graph representing the road network, we need to match a very few positioning data points to single points on the map, corresponding to the bus stops. Some studies related to the bus domain addressed slightly different problems. For example, Li, in [32], proposed an algorithm to align bus stops to the road network.

A first technique to achieve this could be, for a given route, to find the bus stop $rs = (rs_x, rs_y)$ that minimises the euclidean distance from the geographical point $P = (P_x, P_y)$ collected from the GNSS, relative to the considered entry, as shown in Fig. 4. However, when applying this procedure to our context, a problem may arise: the nearest stop, based on euclidean distance, may be on the same route but in the opposite leg, w.r.t the one the vehicle is heading (see Fig. 5). Such a mismatch can be corrected by considering the direction of travel of the vehicle, which can be easily derived. In this way, it is possible to correct the assigned stop, replacing it with the corresponding one on the correct leg.

From our experience, the process of bus stop matching is thus not trivial, as it requires also knowledge on the line and the stops that constitute it, as well as reasoning on the plausibility of the path made, in order to correct any errors.

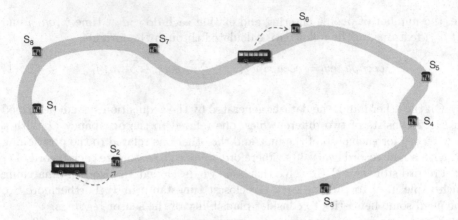

Fig. 4. Bus stop matching.

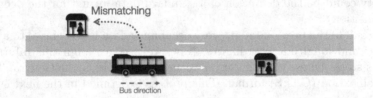

Fig. 5. A mismatch example.

Aggregation by Time Slots. As described in Sect. 3, crowding data are not sampled with a fixed frequency but according to asynchronous events. Since most time series models assume that data come from observations that are equally spaced in time [33], it could be useful to aggregate data by time windows of fixed size α. Different aggregation strategies can be used. We adopted the mean value of each slot as representative one. Choosing the window size is also a challenge, as the higher its value, the smaller the size of the data set. Vice versa the smaller its value, the greater the presence of missing data. Thus, the window size must be set according to the frequency with whom buses pass at the considered stop, which can be very different from stop to stop, as Fig. 6 shows. A possible way to make this choice is to define the window size considering the average number of times buses pass by a given stop.

5   The Prediction Phase: Challenges and Experiences

In the KDD process, after the preprocessing phase, data should be transformed to be used as input for the data mining phase. We do not report any significant challenge in the transformation phase, rather focusing on the mining one. In detail, for BPL prediction, time series forecasting techniques are applied to predict the future occupancy of vehicles passing at the stop rs, for each stop s

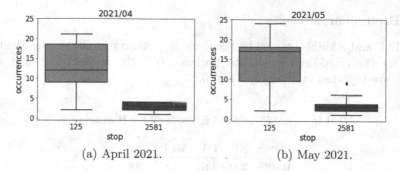

(a) April 2021.   (b) May 2021.

Fig. 6. Comparison between number of bus passages at stop 125 and stop 2581, in the same months

of a given route r. In other terms, we are willing to predict what would be the BPL for the next three buses passing by a given stop of a given route.

5.1   The Experimental Protocol

To understand which mining technique is more suitable, we need to assess the prediction performance of the trained models. Let us note that, in the present paper, BPL prediction is set as a regression problem, because the intent is to predict the *number* of people on-board the vehicle. As done by similar work (*e.g.* [7,27]), some appropriate metrics for this task are *Mean Absolute Error (MAE)* and *Root Mean Square Error (RMSE)*, defined as follows:

$$MAE = \frac{1}{n} \sum_{i=1}^{n} |e_i| \qquad (2)$$

$$RMSE = \sqrt{\frac{1}{n} \sum_{i=1}^{n} e_i^2} \qquad (3)$$

Given these metrics, we applied three machine/deep learning techniques for the generation of regression models, which are different for "power" and computational costs, namely:

- Regression tree (**RT**);
- Multilayer Perceptron (**MLP**), with one hidden layer of 100 neurons;
- Long Short-Term Memory (**LSTM**) network, with one layer of 32 neurons.

The dataset was divided using the 70% of the days, selected in the selection phase, for the training set, the 15% for the validation set and the remaining 15% for the test set. The BPL predictions produced by these models are then compared with a *baseline* we defined, *i.e.* the *Naive Forecasting* [34] (**NF** in the following), where the predicted value at instant $t + ho$ is equal to the observed value at instant t:

$$Occupancy_{t+ho} = Occupancy_t \qquad (4)$$

5.2   Preliminary Results

The MAE and RMSE obtained by the three regression techniques plus the baselines, for the considered prediction horizons (i.e. the BPL of the next three buses), are reported in Tables 1, 2 and 3.

Table 1. RMSE and MAE obtained for Horizon = 1

Metric	NF	DT	MLP	LSTM
RMSE	3.85	3.64	3.53	3.58
MAE	2.45	2.22	2.34	2.23

Table 2. RMSE and MAE obtained for Horizon = 2

Metric	NF	DT	MLP	LSTM
RMSE	5.57	5.06	4.85	4.75
MAE	3.91	3.64	3.62	3.40

Table 3. RMSE and MAE obtained for horizon=3

Metric	NF	DT	MLP	LSTM
RMSE	6.79	6.00	6.04	5.44
MAE	4.92	4.45	4.83	4.08

The Absolute Error (AE) box plots, at different horizon values, are shown in Fig. 7. It can be observed that none of the models trained with the three methods is able to outperform the baseline, even in the case of the deep learning technique.

Further comparisons are made by checking for any statistically significant differences, by means of the *Wilcoxon-signed rank sum test*, with $p = 0.05$. Given these settings, we found that no statistically significant differences between machine learning techniques and the baseline can be found, for any of the considered horizon. Thus, even in presence of state of the art regression technique (*e.g.* LSTM) the prediction accuracy obtained with the regression models is comparable with the one achievable by the very simple baseline. To understand why advanced prediction methods are performing so poorly, we focused our attention on the raw occupancy data, for each stop of the considered route.

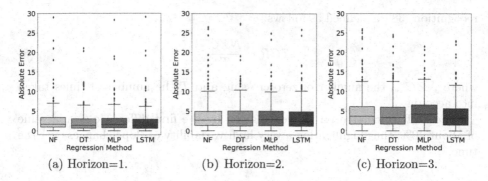

(a) Horizon=1.

(b) Horizon=2.

(c) Horizon=3.

Fig. 7. Boxplots of the absolute errors of the different regression techniques, with the considered prediction horizons.

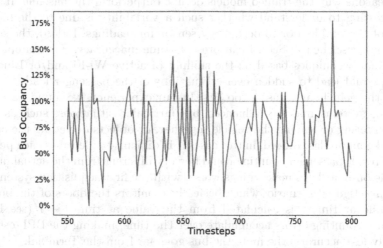

Fig. 8. An example of the dynamics of the raw data: bus occupancy recorded at a stop. The horizontal line represents the maximum capacity of the bus

An example of plot of the collected raw data is shown in Fig. 8, where we report the BPLs (in percentage w.r.t. the total capacity of bus) that were measured over the time at a given bus stop. From this Figure we can observe that the collected data are characterised by high variability (*e.g.* large and frequent jumps). It is well recognised that a signal with strong, abrupt and frequent changes from one sampling instant to the other can pose problems to regression algorithms, as it makes it difficult for a model to identify the underlying trend, worsening its generalizability performances (*e.g.* [35,36]).

For a more accurate quantification of such signal variability, we computed its Zero Crossing Rate (ZCR), *i.e.* a measure of the rate of sign change of the first derivative (zero crossing) of a signal over the time, which gives an indication of how often the signal changes direction. This metric, widely used in domains which deal with noisy signals, such as the acoustic signals analysis [37] or speech recognition [38], is defined as follows:

$$ZCR = \frac{NZC}{T} \tag{5}$$

where NZC is the number of zero crossing and T the number of times taken into account.

The ZCR calculated on the series given by the first difference gave a value of about 40%, thus highlighting a very high variability of slope changes over the time.

Discussion and Open Research Challenges. The dynamics of the collected data, with this significant number of variability and abrupt changes, could be one of the reasons why the trained models do not outperform the baseline. It would be interesting to understand whether such a variability is due to the intrinsic nature of the problem or to occupancy sensor misreadings. Indeed, the sensing techniques described in Sect. 4 can present some inaccuracy. For example, it is known that techniques based on the sniffing of active Wi-Fi and/or Bluetooth devices, could lead to sudden over-estimations of the passenger load if devices outside the vehicle are sensed, too [39]. In our experience, we found that video recording systems may be influenced by particular situations, such as many people entering or leaving the vehicle together, or objects occluding the camera views, like umbrellas. Indeed, in this cases it is difficult to identifies each persons, and the result passenger counting could be very different from the actual number of people on-board. To make things worse, with the first acquisition system used in the investigated scenario, which basically monitors the doors of the bus, the BPL value at time t is calculated from the value at time $t - 1$ (see Eq. 1). Therefore, counting errors accumulate over the time, making the BPL estimate gradually less accurate, the more the bus goes far from the Terminal.

We speculate that the application of more advanced data preprocessing techniques, including a smoothing step, as done in presence of similar data dynamics (*e.g.* [36]), could be useful to improve prediction performance.

6   Conclusions

The ability to perform accurate Bus Passenger Load predictions is very relevant in urban scenarios, to obtain better route planning/scheduling, higher comfort for commuters, and, in times of on-going pandemics, to achieve a more effective on-board social distancing. Nevertheless, to date the number of data-driven studies on BPL predictions is still limited, mostly due to the difficulties in collecting proper datasets.

Within an industry-academia partnership, we are developing a Urban Mobility solution based on a BPL predictor for a major Italian city. This solution is based on a typical *Knowledge Discovery in Database* (KDD) pipeline, applied on crowding data collected from about two dozens of buses. In this paper we have reported some experiences on the instantiation of a KDD pipeline for BPL prediction. In details, the data preprocessing and the mining steps have turned out to be particularly challenging, due to the different data formats, collected from different sensing solutions, to issues in the bus stop matching phase, and above all in the prediction phase. In particular, even deep learning based techniques were not able to provide BPL predictions whose performance outperforms the trivial baseline we defined in a statistically significant way. It would be interesting to assess whether the use of some smoothing techniques, capable of dealing with the abrupt changes in the data we found, could be beneficial to improve the prediction performances.

We hope that the scientific community in the field of spatio-temporal data management could define standards, techniques, and solutions able to relieve practitioners willing to develop solutions like the one we described.

References

1. Kirimtat, A., Krejcar, O., Kertesz, A., Tasgetiren, M.F.: Future trends and current state of smart city concepts: a survey. IEEE Access **8**, 86448–86467 (2020)
2. Paiva, S., Ahad, M.A., Tripathi, G., Feroz, N., Casalino, G.: Enabling technologies for urban smart mobility: recent trends, opportunities and challenges. Sensors **21**(6), 2143 (2021)
3. Gavalas, D., et al.: Smart cities: recent trends, methodologies, and applications (2017)
4. Zear, A., Singh, P.K., Singh, Y.: Intelligent transport system: a progressive review (2016)
5. Tirachini, A., Hensher, D.A., Rose, J.M.: Crowding in public transport systems: effects on users, operation and implications for the estimation of demand. Transp. Res. Part A Policy Pract. **53**, 36–52 (2013)
6. Kim, K.M., Hong, S.-P., Ko, S.-J., Kim, D.: Does crowding affect the path choice of metro passengers? Transp. Res. Part A Policy Pract. **77**, 292–304 (2015)
7. Wang, P., Chen, X., Chen, J., Hua, M., Pu, Z.: A two-stage method for bus passenger load prediction using automatic passenger counting data. IET Intel. Transport Syst. **15**(2), 248–260 (2021)
8. Tsai, T.-H.: Self-evolutionary sibling models to forecast railway arrivals using reservation data. Eng. Appl. Artif. Intell. **96**, 103960 (2020)
9. Bin, Y., Zhongzhen, Y., Baozhen, Y.: Bus arrival time prediction using support vector machines. J. Intell. Transp. Syst. **10**(4), 151–158 (2006)
10. Yu, B., Lam, W.H., Tam, M.L.: Bus arrival time prediction at bus stop with multiple routes. Transp. Res. Part C Emerging Technol. **19**(6), 1157–1170 (2011)
11. Jenelius, E.: Data-driven bus crowding prediction based on real-time passenger counts and vehicle locations. In: 6th International Conference on Models and Technologies for Intelligent Transportation Systems (MTITS2019) (2019)
12. Zhang, J., et al.: A real-time passenger flow estimation and prediction method for urban bus transit systems. IEEE Trans. Intell. Transp. Syst. **18**(11), 3168–3178 (2017)
13. Drabicki, A., Kucharski, R., Cats, O., Szarata, A.: Modelling the effects of real-time crowding information in urban public transport systems. Transportmetrica A Transp. Sci. **17**(4), 675–713 (2021)

14. Zhang, Y., Jenelius, E., Kottenhoff, K.: Impact of real-time crowding information: a Stockholm metro pilot study. Public Transp. **9**(3), 483–499 (2017)
15. Ding, H., Taylor, B.D.: Making transit safe to ride during a pandemic: what are the risks and what can be done in response? (2021)
16. Meyer, M.D., Elrahman, O.: Transportation and Public Health: An Integrated Approach to Policy, Planning, and Implementation. Elsevier (2019)
17. Dai, T., Taylor, B.D.: When is public transit too crowded, and how has this changed during the pandemic? (2020)
18. Tirachini, A., Cats, O.: Covid-19 and public transportation: current assessment, prospects, and research needs. J. Public Transp. **22**(1), 1 (2020)
19. Hörcher, D., Singh, R., Graham, D.J.: Social distancing in public transport: mobilising new technologies for demand management under the COVID-19 crisis. Transportation, 1–30 (2021)
20. Gupta, M., Abdelsalam, M., Mittal, S.: Enabling and enforcing social distancing measures using smart city and its infrastructures: a covid-19 use case. arXiv preprint arXiv:2004.09246 (2020)
21. Vandewiele, G.: Predicting train occupancies based on query logs and external data sources. In: Proceedings of the 26th International Conference on World Wide Web Companion, pp. 1469–1474 (2017)
22. Noursalehi, P., Koutsopoulos, H.N., Zhao, J.: Real time transit demand prediction capturing station interactions and impact of special events. Transp. Res. Part C Emerging Technol. **97**, 277–300 (2018)
23. Hu, R., Chiu, Y.-C., Hsieh, C.-W.: Crowding prediction on mass rapid transit systems using a weighted bidirectional recurrent neural network. IET Intel. Transport Syst. **14**(3), 196–203 (2020)
24. Tsai, T.-H., Lee, C.-K., Wei, C.-H.: Neural network based temporal feature models for short-term railway passenger demand forecasting. Expert Syst. Appl. **36**(2), 3728–3736 (2009)
25. Jenelius, E.: Data-driven metro train crowding prediction based on real-time load data. IEEE Trans. Intell. Transp. Syst. **21**(6), 2254–2265 (2019)
26. Arabghalizi, T., Labrinidis, A.: How full will my next bus be? A framework to predict bus crowding levels. In: UrbComp 2019 (2019)
27. Zuo, Z., Yin, W., Yang, G., Zhang, Y., Yin, J., Ge, H.: Determination of bus crowding coefficient based on passenger flow forecasting. J. Adv. Transp. **2019** (2019)
28. Mccarthy, C., et al.: A field study of internet of things-based solutions for automatic passenger counting. IEEE Open J. Intell. Transp. Syst. **2**, 384–401 (2021)
29. Seidel, R., Jahn, N., Seo, S., Goerttler, T., Obermayer, K.: NAPC: a neural algorithm for automated passenger counting in public transport on a privacy-friendly dataset. IEEE Open J. Intell. Transp. Syst. **3**, 33–44 (2021)
30. Fayyad, U., Piatetsky-Shapiro, G., Smyth, P.: From data mining to knowledge discovery in databases. AI Mag. **17**(3), 37–37 (1996)
31. Kwoczek, S., Di Martino, S., Nejdl, W.: Stuck around the stadium? An approach to identify road segments affected by planned special events. In: 2015 IEEE 18th International Conference on Intelligent Transportation Systems, pp. 1255–1260. IEEE (2015)
32. Li, J.-Q.: Match bus stops to a digital road network by the shortest path model. Transp. Res. Part C Emerging Technol. **22**, 119–131 (2012)
33. Elorrieta, F., Eyheramendy, S., Palma, W.: Discrete-time autoregressive model for unequally spaced time-series observations. Astronomy Astrophys. **627**, A120 (2019)

34. Chen, R.J., Bloomfield, P., Cubbage, F.W.: Comparing forecasting models in tourism. J. Hospitality Tourism Res. **32**(1), 3–21 (2008)
35. Origlia, A., Di Martino, S., Attanasio, Y.: On-line filtering of on-street parking data to improve availability predictions. In: 2019 6th International Conference on Models and Technologies for Intelligent Transportation Systems (MT-ITS), pp. 1–7. IEEE (2019)
36. Di Martino, S., Origlia, A.: Exploiting recurring patterns to improve scalability of parking availability prediction systems. Electronics **9**(5), 838 (2020)
37. Gouyon, F., Pachet, F., Delerue, O., et al.: On the use of zero-crossing rate for an application of classification of percussive sounds. In: Proceedings of the COST G-6 Conference on Digital Audio Effects (DAFX-00), Verona, Italy, vol. 5. Citeseer (2000)
38. Ito, M., Donaldson, R.: Zero-crossing measurements for analysis and recognition of speech sounds. IEEE Trans. Audio Electroacoust. **19**(3), 235–242 (1971)
39. Mikkelsen, L., Buchakchiev, R., Madsen, T., Schwefel, H.P.: Public transport occupancy estimation using WLAN probing. In: 2016 8th International Workshop on Resilient Networks Design and Modeling (RNDM), pp. 302–308. IEEE (2016)

On the Impact of Location-related Terms in Neural Embeddings for Content Similarity Measures in Cultural Heritage Recommender Systems

Antonio Origlia and Sergio Di Martino(✉)

University of Naples Federico II, Naples, Italy
{antonio.origlia,sergio.dimartino}@unina.it

Abstract. Analysing text to detect *semantic* similarities is a recent breakthrough of Natural Language Processing that brought many novel applications in different fields. A domain which could greatly benefit of this innovation is the one regarding Location-based and/or Touristic Recommender Systems, where the user receives suggestions based on his/her past liked items. In this work, we consider the use of neural embeddings weighted using Smooth-Inverse Frequency (SIF) to detect semantic similarities in textual descriptions found in a large graph database covering Italian cultural Points of Interests (POIs). Of all detected similar pairs on a national scale, 19% are composed by POIs that do not belong to the same ontological category, highlighting the potential neural embeddings have to match POIs beyond the categories they have been assigned to. However, since text descriptions also contain references to the places where POIs are found, similarities can be detected among POIs sharing the same location, especially in the case of low-frequency geographical terms. While this may be desirable, in some cases, it may harm location-aware applications, as POIs positions are already known. By comparing city names occurrence probabilities both in the full text corpus and in location-constrained sub-corpora, we observed probability shifts, on average, of 232%. This suggests that, for the specific case of location-aware services, SIF-weighted neural embeddings should use location-constrained sub-corpora for term occurrence probability computation in order to efficiently remove uninteresting information.

Keywords: Neural embeddings · Location-based services · Semantic analysis

1 Introduction

The World Wide Web represent an excellent resource for users willing to plan touristic/cultural activities, especially at unknown destination. However, the list of possibilities offered by Web search engines (or even specialised tourism sites) may be overwhelming, and more advanced solutions to filter relevant information are required [3]. Recommender systems (RSs) are tools able to search and

© Springer Nature Switzerland AG 2022
F. Karimipour and S. Storandt (Eds.): W2GIS 2022, LNCS 13238, pp. 108–120, 2022.
https://doi.org/10.1007/978-3-031-06245-2_10

filter relevant information to provide suggestions to user about concepts/items of their interest, based on their preferences, restrictions or tastes [20]. A lot of research efforts have been aimed at refining even more the quality of the suggested options, giving rise to a wide discipline (e.g.: [24]), including solutions based on collaborative scenarios (the user gets suggestions based actions of other *similar* users), content-based analyses, or hybrid approaches. If we restrict our focus on Content-based RSs, we notice that with these solutions, the user will be recommended items that are similar to the ones (s)he liked in the past [24]. Here, the definition of *similarity* among items is the key point. In particular, (Location-Based) RSs can take great advantage from state-of-the-art text processing techniques. For example, a system could suggest Points of Interests (POIs) potentially relevant for a user, given an analysis of the textual description of other POIs he/she previously liked.

Recent developments in text processing through the use of deep neural networks led to significant breakthroughs in a number of different fields. In particular, *neural embeddings* have boosted the capability to represent text semantics, with significant improvements over older Information Retrieval techniques, mostly based on term frequency like TF-IDF [2]. Text embeddings, in general, are vector-based representations of natural language texts that capture *semantics* by analysing words in the context they occur and, scaling up, sentences and documents. Bidirectional Encoder Representations from Transformers (BERT) models [7], in particular, have become the reference model to obtain semantics representations for computational application. The BERT architecture and its variants consist of a Transformer Deep Neural Network (DNN) [21], trained on the language modelling tasks. Transformers consist of a sequence of *Encoder* modules designed to learn a compact representation of the input and of a sequence of *Decoder* modules designed to build the desired output from this representation. Neural embeddings consist of the output obtained from the last Encoder in the trained model. Decoders are, therefore, only needed during the training phase and are, then, discarded. For the specific case of language modelling with BERT, the training task consists of learning to predict randomly *masked* words in an input sequence. Neural embeddings have strong applications for query/document matching for the case of search engines (e.g. [5]), entity alignment for POIs [25] and question answering [11], even specifically related to spatial-related queries [22]. Advanced visual interface for Cultural Heritage, can also make use of text-based matching [6]. When, for example, 3D models are semantically annotated [4,13], searches for similar items can make use of this kind of information from unstructured data.

Nevertheless, text similarity, for the case of POI descriptions, can be strongly influenced by location-related topics. This can be desirable in some cases, like for entity alignment, while for the case of location-aware services, this kind of information may not be relevant, being intrinsically available with good precision, as with GPS. In this paper, we present a methodology based on the use of neural embeddings to detect similarities among Italian cultural POIs based on their descriptions. We use a weighting schema designed to remove common *topics* from a corpus of documents obtained from Wikipedia in order to maximise the discriminative power of the semantic representation. Then, we show that, in a significant number of cases, textual similarity allows to detect site pairs across the ontological categories imported from Wikidata. Since the weighting procedure is influenced by word occurrence probabilities in the reference corpus, we also present an in-depth analysis to analyse the difference between location-specific sub-corpora and the entire dataset. We show how constraining the text used for term probability computation to material extracted with location-aware queries produces very different results in the probabilities used for weighting. This is mainly caused by terms describing relatively small areas, like town names, being very frequent in the constrained corpus and very rare in the entire corpus. In this sense, the importance of location-related terms may be overweighted, when computing description similarities, producing biases towards site pairs that are simply found in the same place but do not share any other similarity. From this, we conclude that, depending on whether or not location-related semantic information is useful for the considered technological applications, different weighting schemas should be adopted to either keep or remove location-related semantic information.

Summarising, our main contributions are:

- an analysis of POIs similarities detected from text and their relationship with ontological categorisation;
- an analysis of the difference between using location-related corpora and the full dataset on the adopted weighting schema.

The rest of the paper is organised as follows: in Sect. 2 we describe the database from which we extracted the data used in our evaluation, Sect. 3 presents the neural embeddings extraction procedure, discussing the weighting schema that motivates the investigation. Section 4 contains the result of the analysis conducted on cultural POIs descriptions extracted from the database.

2 Material

In this Section, we present the dataset from which we extract textual descriptions and locations for Italian cultural heritage sites, representing the case study we consider for our analysis.

2.1 Data Sources

Handling massive amounts of data can pose several issues to standard relational solutions [8,9]. The base material is constituted by a graph database representing Italian cultural heritage POIs integrated with social network activity collected from Flickr. The database is described in detail in [17] and it contains approximately 690 k nodes and more than 2 M relationships. The collection procedure was designed to integrate massive information coming from Linked Open Data

(LOD) with popularity scores coming from Flickr pictures and relevance scores obtained by considering a set of linguistic measures computed on the Italian pages linked to the sites of interest. We summarise here the collection procedure and the database structure, which is further extended in this work.

The database assembling procedure is composed of the following steps:

1. **Data ingestion**: this involves sources selection and design of the unified representation in such a way that the original structure is still preserved while not interfering with other sources;
2. **Data enrichment**: this involves applying data processing techniques that can be executed offline to record, in the database, the results of data processing techniques to support subsequent analyses;
3. **Data analysis**: this involves the deployment stage, where represented and enriched data are queried to infer conclusions based on the combination of information coming from the different sources through a single interface.

During the data ingestion step, a starting graph is obtained by replicating the structure, described in RDF, found in LOD. As LOD are largely available in the cultural heritage domain (e.g. Wikidata, the Art and Architecture Thesarurus, Europeana, etc....), it is plausible to consider these well-established structured resources as a reference to support this first step. The representational power of graph databases makes it possible to design a dedicated sub-graph for each of the considered unstructured data sources, which may be linked to the basic structure using cross-domain relationships. This is the case, for example, of text data collected from Wikipedia pages linked to cultural POIs, where the organisation into sections was used to create *deepening trees* representing the complexity of the topics related to the site itself. Lastly, an estimate of the POIs' popularity was provided by collecting pictures from the Flickr social network.

The amount of geo-referenced pictures that could be linked to the sites of interest depending on the pictures tags and descriptions represented the popularity of the site during the data enrichment phase, which includes data analysis techniques aimed at extracting deeper knowledge from the data collected from the previous step. Considered measures at this step include the PageRank score of cultural POIs considering social activity from Flickr users and lexical complexity measures aimed at further detailing the content of the Wikipedia pages describing cultural POIs.

Data analysis revealed that the collected resource was consistent with respect to seasonal patterns, that it could be used to evaluate the balance between the complexity of the geo-referenced text and the amount of social activity detected from Flickr and that it was able to highlight the connections between cultural POIs by analysing co-occurrences in visiting patterns among visitors. In this paper, we further detail visitors behaviour using the collected database and we report on new insights we gained, which extend the potential applications of the database.

2.2   Database Structure

The database is implemented in Neo4j [23], an open source graph database manager that has been developed over the last 16 years and applied to a high number of tasks related to data representation [10], exploration [12] and visualisation [14]. Neo4j is characterised by high scalability, ease of use and its proprietary query language: Cypher. Cypher is designed to be a *declarative* language that highlights patterns' structure using an SQL-inspired *ASCII-art syntax*.

The graph resulting from the previously described assembling procedure is composed by nodes and relationships among nodes. Node labels represent different items in the domain like, for example, FLICKRUSERs, PICTUREs and SITEs. SITEs also have secondary labels to further specify the typology of the site. The considered labels are mapped onto Wikidata categories as follows:

- Museum (wd:Q33506)
- Archaeological Site (wd:Q839954)
- Palace (wd:Q16560)
- Monument (wd:Q4989906)
- Sacred Architecture (wd:Q47848)
- Protected Area (wd:Q473972)

Concerning textual material related to cultural POIs, the database contains English and Italian descriptions obtained from Wikipedia and organised into a *deepening tree*, reflecting the structure of the Wikipedia page to represent, through the graph, the complexity of the information organisation. In this work, we consider the entire descriptions available for POI similarity detection while including text deepening levels is left for future work. Figure 1 shows the graph database structure.

3   Text Analysis

In this Section, we describe the procedure used to extract neural embeddings from the Wikipedia texts describing cultural POIs found in Italy.

3.1   Embeddings

Representing text semantics as numeric vectors is a powerful technique to capture similarities between documents. The basic concept comes from the distributional semantics field, leveraging on the observation that words occurring in the same context tend to have similar meanings. The method which paved the way for the recent developments in representing text semantics using numerical vectors is represented by word2vec [16], where word embeddings were computed in a context-independent way: that is, in word2vec, each word in a given corpus is assigned a numerical vector. This is obtained either by training a simple feedforward neural network in predicting the current word given its context (CBOW

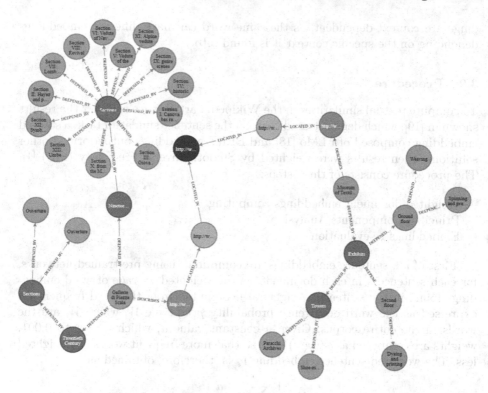

Fig. 1. Database structure. Cultural POIs (orange) linked to two different CITY nodes (yellow) by LOCATED_IN relationships, which also link CITY nodes to the same REGION (brown). Deepening trees containing textual descriptions are constituted by CONCRETE (green) nodes, containing actual text and by ABSTRACT (purple) nodes, containing (sub-)section data. (Color figure online)

architecture) or by predicting the context given the word (Skip-Gram architecture). The word probability distributions given an input word that are returned by the network trained with one-hot vectors representing words constitute the embedding. Word2vec is, therefore, context-independent in the sense that words are assigned a single embedding and meaning similarity is computed using cosine similarity in general. This poses a problem where the same word can have a different meaning in different contexts.

The most widely used neural embeddings, nowadays, are BERT embeddings [7] and they have been intensively applied, in the last years, to a large number of case studies where Natural Language Processing techniques could be applied. Neural embeddings are obtained by training a Transformer Deep Neural Network in predicting a set of *masked* words in a large text corpus. After training, embeddings are obtained as the output of the Encoder section of the Transformer, given an input sentence. Being provided at sentence-level, neural embeddings are context-dependent, as the same word can have different embeddings depending on the specific context it is found into.

3.2 Procedure

To compute textual similarities in the Wikipedia articles, we consider the results shown in [19], which demonstrated that, on the sentence similarity task, a stacked embedding composed of ELMo [18] and BERT embeddings outperformed other solutions when results were weighted by Smooth Inverse Frequency (SIF) [1]. The procedure consists of three steps:

– Weighted document embeddings computing
– Principal Components Analysis
– Embeddings re-evaluation

First of all, sentence embeddings are computed, using pre-trained networks, for each sentence s in each document, as the weighted average of word embeddings found in the sentence. Weights are computed from the word frequencies, expressed as the word occurrence probability $p(w) : w \in W$ where W are the words in the entire corpus. Given a constant value a, which we set to 0.001, weights are computed as $a/(p(w)+a)$, so that more frequent words are weighted less. The weighted sentence embedding v_s is, therefore, obtained as

$$v_s = \frac{1}{|s|} \sum_{w \in s} \frac{a}{a + p(w)} v_w \tag{1}$$

Document embeddings v_d are obtained by considering the average of the sentence embeddings $v_s : s \in d$ and $d \in D$ where D is the set of all documents. After computing document embeddings, we consider the X matrix whose columns are the v_d embeddings. The final embedding $\bar{v}_d$ is obtained by subtracting, from each v_d, the first principal component of the X matrix. This removes, from the semantic representation, elements that are common to all the documents, leaving the traits with actual discriminative power in the data.

In this specific case, we compute semantic representations of the considered pages using stacked embeddings of ELMo and RoBERTa [15] embeddings, which build upon BERT embeddings and have been shown to produce better results. For each pair of document embeddings related to pages that do not describe the same site, similarity is computed as the cosine of the two SIF-weighted embeddings. A SIMILAR_TO relationship is, then, established in the database between the two POIs. The SIMILAR_TO relationship has a *degree* property containing the cosine between the two SIF-weighted stacked embeddings.

4 Results

While similarity degrees are computed for all pairs of documents in the corpus, for our analyses, we only consider pairs of POIs (s_1, s_2) having a similarity degree

$s_{deg} > 0.9$ to concentrate on the closest document pairs, from a semantic content point of view. These pairs, together with the Wikidata ontological labels, can be extracted from the database using the following query:

```
MATCH (s1:SITE)-[r:SIMILAR_TO]->(s2:SITE) WHERE r.degree > 0.9
RETURN DISTINCT s1, s2,
[x in labels(s1) WHERE NOT x in
['SITE', 'MAINSITE', 'ESTIMATEDPOSITION']] AS labels1,
[x in labels(s2) WHERE NOT x in
['SITE', 'MAINSITE', 'ESTIMATEDPOSITION']] AS labels2
```

There are approximately 18,400 (s_1, s_2) pairs in the database, matching this query. First of all, we verify that document embeddings are not simply capturing ontological categories that are already available in the database, as part of the Wikidata import procedure. By extracting, from the considered set of pairs, all the ones having at least one different label, we observed that they constitute 19% of the cases, indicating that, while in the majority of the cases similar POIs also belong to the same ontological class, the procedure is not merely matching known categories. The query to extract this subset of data is the following:

```
MATCH (s1:SITE)-[r:SIMILAR_TO]->(s2:SITE)<-[:DESCRIBES]-(:ROOT)
-[:DEEPENED_BY*]->(n1:CONCRETE) WHERE r.degree > 0.9
WITH [x in labels(s1) WHERE x in labels(s2)
AND NOT x in ['SITE', 'MAINSITE', 'ESTIMATEDPOSITION']]
AS intersection, [x in labels(s1)
WHERE NOT x in ['SITE', 'MAINSITE', 'ESTIMATEDPOSITION']]
AS labels1, [x in labels(s2)
WHERE NOT x in ['SITE', 'MAINSITE', 'ESTIMATEDPOSITION']]
AS labels2, s1, s2 WHERE isEmpty(intersection)
RETURN DISTINCT s1.WikiID, s2.WikiID, labels1, labels2
```

To better characterise this, we analyse label co-occurrences shown in the heatmap reported in Fig. 2.

For the case of Italian cultural heritage, SACRED_BUILDINGs constitute the majority, so most of the semantic similarities in text descriptions involve this kind of cultural POIs. An exception is constituted by PROTECTED_AREAs, which are lower in number with respect to the other categories and do not constitute built heritage, being mostly natural parks. The observed differences between SACRED_BUILDINGs and PROTECTED_AREAs is, therefore, expected. Another strong correspondence is constituted by MUSEUM and PALACE pairs: in many cases, Italian museums are hosted inside buildings that constitute heritage *per se*, so the correspondence is expected in this case, too.

Given the potential provided by semantic analysis to bridge over ontological categories, we proceed to a closer inspection of the matched items with a focus on location-based services, concentrating on matched POIs that are found in the same city and have different labels. These are extracted, from the database, using the following query:

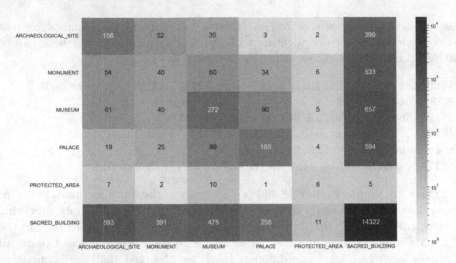

Fig. 2. Labels co-occurrences for site pairs having cosine similarity $s_{deg} > 0.9$.

```
MATCH (c:CITY)<-[:LOCATED_IN]-(s1:SITE)-[r:SIMILAR_TO]
->(s2:SITE)-[:LOCATED_IN]->(c) WHERE r.degree > 0.9
WITH [x in labels(s1) WHERE NOT x in labels(s2)
AND NOT x in ['SITE', 'MAINSITE', 'ESTIMATEDPOSITION']]
AS intersection, [x in labels(s1) WHERE NOT x in
['SITE', 'MAINSITE', 'ESTIMATEDPOSITION']] AS labels1,
[x in labels(s2) WHERE NOT x in
['SITE', 'MAINSITE', 'ESTIMATEDPOSITION']] AS labels2,
s1, s2 WHERE isEmpty(intersection)
RETURN DISTINCT s1.WikiID, s2.WikiID, labels1, labels2
```

By removing the constraint concerning site pairs having different labels, we compute the total number of POIs that can be semantically related. Then, we observe that (s_1, s_2) pairs bridging over categories constitute 17% of the cases, once again not being neglectable. Using SIF-weighted embeddings to identify POIs that have semantically similar descriptions for location-based services, however, poses a risk linked to the need to compute $p(w)$, since geolocalised texts have a higher probability to contain systematic references to the surrounding area where they are found. This has the potential effect, for embedding-based methods, to capture similarities in the descriptions that simply refer, for example, to the city where the cultural site is located: SIF-weighting based on probabilities computed over the global corpus would not remove this information which would actually be useful in non-geolocalised texts. For this specific case, however, the risk is to detect similarities caused by an *uninteresting* similarity. To estimate the potential impact of this issue, we consider the texts describing matched cultural POIs found in the same CITY, in the database. These are extracted using the following query:

```
MATCH (c:CITY)<-[:LOCATED_IN]-(s1:SITE)-[r:SIMILAR_TO]
->(s2:SITE)-[:LOCATED_IN]->(c)
WHERE r.degree > 0.9 WITH c,
COLLECT(s1.WikiID) + COLLECT(s2.WikiID) AS list
UNWIND list as site RETURN DISTINCT c.name AS city,
COLLECT(DISTINCT site) AS sites
```

We, then, consider the probabilities to observe the name of each returned CITY with respect to the probability of observing the same name in the whole set of descriptions of matched POIs. The probability increase when switching from global probabilities to local probabilities is, on average, of 232%. POIs found in smaller towns, in particular, are more likely to be considered similar, as the CITY name is considerably less frequent, in the global corpus, with respect to the corresponding local one. The full report is shown in Table 1. This suggests that, for location based services based on semantic similarities among geolocalised texts available in LODs, for the case of cultural POIs, it may be important to remove localisation-related information from the actual comparisons, as they may not be relevant and mask more interesting relationships.

As a practical application scenario, let's consider the case of location-aware POI recommendation, like for example cultural sites. Travelling users may query for sites similar to the last one they visited and, other than considering ontological relationships, search engines are now able to use semantic matching based on descriptive texts. However, there is a risk that text embeddings trained on a large corpus of cultural sites descriptions capture location-based text similarities, as they are indeed present in text descriptions and they also represent, in general, a possible way to match cultural sites. On this basis, the engine may, therefore, recommend close sites just because they are in the same city and not because they share, for example, architectural styles or historical characters linked to their history. In this case, the information, included in the description text, that the two sites are in the same place is already known by the system through GPS and is, therefore, not an important point of view for semantic matching. To remove location-based semantic information from the embeddings used for semantic matching, training with location-constrained sub-corpora may yield more reliable results as the procedure would remove topics that are related to information that is included in the text but is irrelevant for the service.

Table 1. Global city name observation probabilities from descriptions of strongly similar POIs compared with with observation probabilities from descriptions limited to POIs LOCATED_IN the same CITY. Percentage increase is also reported.

City	Local Probability	Global Probability	Change (%)
Todi	0,167	5,23E-05	3188,208
Roccamorice	0,033	5,23E-05	631,570
Serramonacesca	0,031	5,23E-05	601,685
Pescara	0,069	1,57E-04	438,891
Fiesole	0,031	7,84E-05	395,175
Ragusa	0,011	3,92E-05	270,422
Parma	0,010	3,92E-05	266,159
Grosseto	0,050	1,96E-04	254,990
Fermo	0,023	1,05E-04	220,473
Palermo	0,068	3,40E-04	200,291
Piacenza	0,013	7,84E-05	158,460
Modena	0,013	9,15E-05	138,470
Pescia	0,009	6,53E-05	131,653
Lucca	0,018	1,70E-04	106,213
Bergamo	0,007	7,84E-05	90,120
Mantua	0,025	2,87E-04	84,753
Cefalù	0,008	1,05E-04	78,153
Turin	0,009	1,44E-04	59,507
Cortona	0,009	1,96E-04	47,010
Siena	0,010	2,09E-04	45,176
Pisa	0,022	5,10E-04	41,696
Verona	0,021	5,23E-04	38,396
Genoa	0,026	7,45E-04	34,195
Brugherio	0,010	3,27E-04	30,369
Milan	0,017	6,66E-04	24,712
Assisi	0,015	6,01E-04	24,044
Bologna	0,010	4,18E-04	23,781
Venice	0,019	1,10E-03	16,655
Alcamo	0,018	1,19E-03	13,999
Padua	0,011	7,58E-04	13,506
Naples	0,015	1,57E-03	8,847
Florence	0,010	1,15E-03	7,289
Rome	0,010	4,17E-03	1,496

5   Conclusions

In this paper, we have investigated the use of neural embeddings and, in particular, the impact of location-related terms on a weighting schema designed to increase the discriminative power of the obtained vectors. SIF-weighting, in particular, is performed using term occurrence probabilities over the considered corpus. We have shown that a procedure based on this measure can be sensitive to location-related terms. While this may be desirable for tasks like entity matching, semantic analysis for location-aware services can suffer from this aspect. Specifically, detecting similarities between POIs because their description contains references to the place they are found is irrelevant when the location is already known through GPS. In these cases, removing the sensitivity to location-related similarities may provide advantages. Future work will explore this topic more in depth to further detail the effect of SIF-weighting neural embeddings using location-constrained sub-corpora instead of the full dataset.

References

1. Arora, S., Liang, Y., Ma, T.: A simple but tough-to-beat baseline for sentence embeddings. In: Proceedings of the 5th International Conference on Learning Representations (2017)
2. Baeza-Yates, R., Ribeiro-Neto, B., et al.: Modern Information Retrieval, vol. 463. ACM press New York (1999)
3. Borràs, J., Moreno, A., Valls, A.: Intelligent tourism recommender systems: a survey. Expert Syst. Appl. **41**(16), 7370–7389 (2014)
4. Cera, V., Origlia, A., Cutugno, F., Campi, M.: Semantically annotated 3d material supporting the design of natural user interfaces for architectural heritage. In: AVI* CH (2018)
5. Dai, Z., Callan, J.: Deeper text understanding for ir with contextual neural language modeling. In: Proceedings of the 42nd International ACM SIGIR Conference on Research and Development in Information Retrieval, pp. 985–988 (2019)
6. De Carolis, B.N., Gena, C., Kuflik, T., Origlia, A., Raptis, G.E.: AVI-CH 2018: advanced visual interfaces for cultural heritage. In: Proceedings of the 2018 International Conference on Advanced Visual Interfaces, pp. 1–3 (2018)
7. Devlin, J., Chang, M.W., Lee, K., Toutanova, K.: Bert: pre-training of deep bidirectional transformers for language understanding. arXiv preprint arXiv:1810.04805 (2018)
8. Di Martino, S., Fiadone, L., Peron, A., Riccabone, A., Vitale, V.N.: Industrial internet of things: persistence for time series with nosql databases. In: 2019 IEEE 28th International Conference on Enabling Technologies: Infrastructure for Collaborative Enterprises (WETICE), pp. 340–345. IEEE (2019)
9. Di Martino, S., Peron, A., Riccabone, A., Vitale, V.N.: Benchmarking management techniques for massive IIoT time series in a fog architecture. Int. J. Grid. Util. Comput. **12**(2), 113–125 (2021)
10. Dietze, F., Karoff, J., Calero Valdez, A., Ziefle, M., Greven, C., Schroeder, U.: An open-source object-graph-mapping framework for neo4j and Scala: Renesca. In: Buccafurri, F., Holzinger, A., Kieseberg, P., Tjoa, A.M., Weippl, E. (eds.) CD-ARES 2016. LNCS, vol. 9817, pp. 204–218. Springer, Cham (2016). https://doi.org/10.1007/978-3-319-45507-5_14

11. Do, P., Phan, T.H.V.: Developing a BERT based triple classification model using knowledge graph embedding for question answering system. Appl. Intell. **52**(1), 636–651 (2021). https://doi.org/10.1007/s10489-021-02460-w
12. Drakopoulos, G., Kanavos, A., Makris, C., Megalooikonomou, V.: On converting community detection algorithms for fuzzy graphs in neo4j. In: Proceedings of the 5th International Workshop on Combinations of Intelligent Methods and Applications, CIMA (2015)
13. Grazioso, M., Cera, V., Di Maro, M., Origlia, A., Cutugno, F.: From linguistic linked open data to multimodal natural interaction: a case study. In: 2018 22nd International Conference Information Visualisation (IV), pp. 315–320. IEEE (2018)
14. Jiménez, P., Diez, J.V., Ordieres-Mere, J.: Hoshin kanri visualization with neo4j. empowering leaders to operationalize lean structural networks. Procedia CIRP **55**, 284–289 (2016)
15. Liu, Y., et al.: Roberta: a robustly optimized BERT pretraining approach. arXiv preprint arXiv:1907.11692 (2019)
16. Mikolov, T., Le, Q.V., Sutskever, I.: Exploiting similarities among languages for machine translation. arXiv preprint arXiv:1309.4168 (2013)
17. Origlia, A., Rossi, S., Di Martino, S., Cutugno, F., Chiacchio, M.L.: Multiple-source data collection and processing into a graph database supporting cultural heritage applications. J. Comput. Cult. Heritage (JOCCH) **14**(4), 1–27 (2021)
18. Peters, M.E., et al.: Deep contextualized word representations. arXiv preprint arXiv:1802.05365 (2018)
19. Ranashinghe, T., Orasan, C., Mitkov, R.: Enhancing unsupervised sentence similarity methods with deep contextualised word representations. In: Proceedings of the International Conference on Recent Advances in Natural Language Processing (2019)
20. Ricci, F.: Recommender systems in tourism. In: Xiang Z., Fuchs M., Gretzel U., Höpken W. (eds.) Handbook of e-Tourism, Springer, Cham, pp. 1–18 (2020)
21. Vaswani, A., et al.: Attention is all you need. In: Advances in neural information processing systems, pp. 5998–6008 (2017)
22. Wang, W., Li, Y., Wang, S., Ye, X.: Qa4gis: A novel approach learning to answer GIS developer questions with API documentation. Trans. GIS **25**(5), 2675–2700 (2021)
23. Webber, J.: A programmatic introduction to neo4j. In: Proceedings of the 3rd Annual Conference on Systems, Programming, and Applications: Software for Humanity, pp. 217–218. ACM (2012)
24. Yochum, P., Chang, L., Gu, T., Zhu, M.: Linked open data in location-based recommendation system on tourism domain: a survey. IEEE Access **8**, 16409–16439 (2020)
25. Zhou, C., Zhao, J., Zhang, X., Ren, C.: Entity alignment method of points of interest for internet location-based services. J. Adv. Comput. Intell. Intell. Inf. **24**(7), 837–845 (2020)

Requirements of Voice Indoor Maps for Visually Impaired Persons

Ki-Joune Li(✉)

Pusan National University, Kumjeong-Gu, Pusan 46241, South Korea
lik@pnu.edu
http://lik.pnu.edu

Abstract. With recent progress of indoor positioning technologies and mobile devices, several indoor map and navigation applications have been developed for visually impaired people since 2010s. However there are also several technical challenges for its massive and public utilization. Limited efforts have been done for comprehensive requirement analysis and technical implementations, although a standard, Wayfindr has been published by ITU-F in 2017. In this working-in-progress paper, we analyze requirements for indoor navigation services for visually impaired persons. In particular, we discuss the requirements for verbal user-interface of indoor navigation service for visually impaired persons and its data model. The requirements and design discussed in the paper will be reflected to the development project, called VIM (Voice Indoor Maps), which is a smartphone-based indoor navigation service for visually impaired person.

Keywords: Indoor navigation service for visually impaired person · Indoor voice map · OGC IndoorGML

1 Introduction

Several *Indoor Navigation Services* (INS) have been offered for visually impaired persons (VIP) due to the progress of indoor positioning technologies since 2010. However they are mostly focused on indoor positioning aspects rather than the indoor navigation for VIP without rigorous consideration on the specific requirements for a service for VIP. In order to develop a convenient and helpful INS for VIP, several considerations have to be taken on specific requirements of INS for VIP. First of all, all the instructions are given by audio or verbal ways. It means more than simple giving verbal instructions but implies verbal user-interface. Note that we do not include haptic interface such as vibrations in this paper.

In order to develop a convenient and helpful INS for VIP, we first start from the observation on the difference of INS for VIP from non-VIP. Second, we

This work was supported by BK21PLUS and a grant (21NSIP-B135746-05) from National Spatial Information Research Program (NSIP) funded by MOLIT of Korean government.

F. Karimipour and S. Storandt (Eds.): W2GIS 2022, LNCS 13238, pp. 121–130, 2022.
https://doi.org/10.1007/978-3-031-06245-2_11

analyze the user requirements of the INS for VIP. Third, we define the functional specifications to fulfill the user requirements. Since most of the developers are non-VIPs, they superficially understand the users requirements. It is critical to fully understand the user requirements and functional requirements for proper development.

Furthermore, these requirements can be also defined for the functional specification and guideline of the development of INS for VIP as a complementary standard of Wayfindr[1], which was also published as ITU-T F.921 standard[2]. It provides a comprehensive functional specification of INS for VIP and has been used as a principal reference for developers as it is the only standard for INS for VIP so far. However we need a more detail requirement analysis and functional specification for the development. In particular, more detail discussion and guideline are needed on how to provide the verbal instructions to users as well as the specification of the indoor maps.

The contributions of this work-in-progress paper are therefore summarized as follows; first, we investigate the requirements and scope of indoor maps. In particular, we discuss the difference between the native data model of IndoorGML, which is an OGC standard for indoor maps, and the model of INS for VIP as an application schema of IndoorGML. Second, we propose a technical guideline of verbal instructions although Wayfindr defined a basic one, particularly on when and which instruction to be given. In Sect. 2, we present the related works and the motivations of the paper. In Sect. 3, we define the basic setups and requirements of INS for VIP. In Sect. 4, we discuss the requirements on the indoor maps and propose an extension of OGC IndoorGML for INS for VIP. We define the specification for the verbal instructions in Sect. 5 and conclude the paper in Sect. 6.

2   Related Works and Motivations

Most works on INS for VIP have been focused on indoor positioning technologies [1–5]. However they require more technical components than indoor positioning for the implementation. Brief technical requirements of INS for VIP are presented beside indoor positioning in [6,7]. And several aspects of verbal navigation services for VIP were also investigated in [10,12]. General approaches for pedestrian navigation service in outdoor space are also presented in [8,9,11]. In particular, it is shown that replacing braille with simple audio-tactile interaction significantly improved efficiency and user satisfaction in [11].

A set of specifications of INS for VIP are defined by Wayfindr as a standard, which includes the basic concepts, requirements, and technical specifications. For this reason, our work starts from the specifications given by Wayfindr. However it stays at an abstract level and does not contain sufficient technical aspects for the implementation. The goal of this paper is to provide more technical

---

[1] https://www.wayfindr.net/ last accessed on 10 Nov. 2021.

[2] https://www.itu.int/ITU-T/recommendations/rec.aspx?rec=13185&lang=en   last accessed on 10 Nov. 2021.

references, which were not discussed in Wayfindr. These technical references will be used for the implementation guidelines of voice indoor maps service, that we are developing for VIP. The issues that are not fully discussed in Wayfindr but included in this paper are summarized as follows;

- Wayfindr does not include the scope and specification of indoor maps. We present the scope of information in indoor maps demanded by INS for VIP and propose its standard model. It should start from the observation on the difference between indoor maps for VIP and non-VIP in terms of INS. In Sect. 3 we will discuss the requirements of indoor maps for VIP in comparison with non-VIP.
- Wayfindr briefly describes how and when to provide verbal instructions to VIP users. Unlike visual presentation of indoor maps and navigation instructions, verbal user-interface of INS for VIP has serious constraints. For example, the verbal user-interface has a limited time interval for giving proper instructions at proper time. We will study the requirements of the verbal user-interface.

In this paper, we therefore discuss these issues and define the functional specifications of the solution that we are developing, called VIM (Voice Indoor Maps).

3   Basic Requirements

In this section, we specify the environment of the target solution that we will analyze and develop. The target solution is a smartphone-based indoor navigation service for visually impaired person with voice assistant user-interface[3]. We assume that VIP users are also assisted by long cane or guide dog for the navigation. We do not assume any specific indoor positioning methods but expect the average accuracy as 2 m that most indoor positioning methods such as BLE, WiFi, and geomagnetic sensors can achieve. Regarding the movement factors of VIP users, we assume one stride 0.85 m and speed 1.4 ms as given in [13].

In brief, there are two approaches for implementing voice indoor maps for VIPs. The first approach is to generate verbal instructions in dynamic ways from indoor maps and the current location. Unlike indoor navigation services for non-VIP, we need an additional step for converting spatial information given by indoor maps to verbal instructions. The second approach is to prepare and register the voice instructions for each position in indoor space. When user arrives at a position, the voice indoor map service searches the corresponding verbal instruction to the position and heading from the instruction table. As it is expensive to prepare all the verbal instructions for every point with different direction of user, we take the first approach for our design and implementation.

The verbal instructions of INS for VIP are classified into three types; instructions on the current location, navigation instructions, and POI (Points of Interest) instructions.

---

[3] TalkBack for Android and VoiceOver for iOS.

The first type of instruction is about the current location, including the verbal description of the current location. Depending on the case of current location, three different types of instructions are given to the user as below;

- Case (a): "On the way from A to B" (Fig. 1-a) instruction when the user is on a way between two named nodes.
- Case (b): "At node C" (Fig. 1-b) when the user is at a named node.
- Case (c): "At intersection M" (Fig. 1-c) when the user is at an intersection.

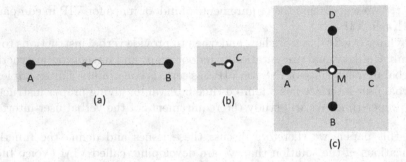

Fig. 1. Three types of instruction for the current location

The second type of verbal instructions is to provide instructions of turn-by-turn navigation. It should include not only turn-by-turn but also preparation instructions. For example, a preparation instruction may be given 2 m before the turning point. The third type of instructions is about POI such as landmarks or safety facilities. In addition to these instruction types, we may provide correction instruction to let the user return back to the correct path, when she/he is deviated from the correct path. The detail of the verbal instructions for each type will be discussed in the Sect. 5.

4   Indoor Maps for VIP Navigation Services

4.1   Base Indoor Maps

OGC IndoorGML is an indoor map standard with the richest expressive power among standard indoor map formats [14]. It is based on *Cellular Space Model*, which assumes an indoor space as a set of non-overlapping cells [15,16] and provides the following features;

- cell geometry,
- cell semantics,
- topology between cells, and
- multi-layered space model.

Due to the rich semantics and extensibility of IndoorGML, we define the data model for VIP navigation in indoor space as an extension from IndoorGML core module. It mainly consists of three parts; topographic part, navigation network, and POI (Points of Interest) for landmarks as shown in Fig. 2.

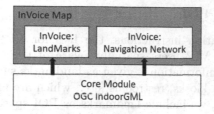

Fig. 2. Data model for VIM as an extension of IndoorGML core module

4.2   Navigation Network

The navigation network of INS for VIP has to be configured for non-visual recognition, while we need geometric information of navigation network for non-VIP users with proper visualization. VIP users are usually aware of their location and space in topological ways, for example by the relative location from the current location. No detail geometry information is required for INS of VIP but the navigation instructions have to be given in terms of the relative location and the direction from the current location. For example, we need geometric information of the network to distinguish the cases given in Fig. 1 of Sect. 3.

The navigation network is to be derived from the topographic indoor map consisting of rooms, hallways, doors, and vertical connections such as elevators and stairs either in automated or manual ways. Since the automated derivation of navigation network is a research topic, we do not discuss it in the paper. Rather we specify the constraints of INS for VIP, which are not found in INS for non-VIP;

- Rectilinear path: In order to provide clear navigation instruction, it is recommended to compute the path has as rectilinear as possible rather than slanted path. For example "turn 30 °C" is more confusing than "turn right".
- Reduce turns: A route with excessive turns makes the navigation difficult and the number of turns has to be reduced as possible.
- Vertical navigation: It is recommended to make the navigation networks via elevators and avoid escalators.
- Evolving doors: It is also recommended to avoid revolving doors, which are dangerous to VIP.

The first and second conditions are conflicting each other and a reasonable compromise has to be found when generating navigation network. It looks difficult to generate the navigation network from a given indoor space in automated way with the consideration of these constraints task. It would be a topic for the future work and we do not discuss it in detail in this paper. As an alternative, we will provide an editing tool for our target solution, which facilitates to draw the navigation network with ease. The navigation network derived from the topographic indoor map is defined as a space layer of multi-layered space model in IndoorGML.

4.3   Landmarks as POIs

In addition to navigation instructions, the INS for VIP should provide the information that lets VIP users spatially aware of their environments. Most of the environmental information is given as landmarks such as nearby vending machines, information kiosks, restrooms, etc., which are all very useful to VIP users. For this reason, we include landmarks as POI space layer on the top of IndoorGML Core Module as depicted by Fig. 2. The landmarks can be prioritized according to its emergency level for the safety measure.

5   Generating and Scheduling Verbal Instructions

An example of verbal instruction given in Appendix A of ITU-F F.921[4], which is an ITU version of Wayfindr, is *"Turn left and take the escalator down to the platforms. The down escalator is the one on the left."* Assuming that it takes 5 s to read the first sentence, the user moves forward 7 m and the second sentence may be no longer valid. This means that verbal message should be as short as possible and given at proper time. In this section, we discuss how to select the verbal instructions and schedule the delivery time.

The verbal instructions are designed depending on three types of instructions explained in Sect. 3. We discuss each type in the subsequent subsections.

5.1   Instruction on the Current Location

As explained in Sect. 3, this function is to provide verbal descriptions of the user's current location. We assume that VIP user stops when she/he listens the instructions on the current location. In addition to the current location, it gives the messages on the direction and nearby landmarks according to the types classified in Fig. 1.

- **case (a)**: *"on the way from B to A"* and nearby landmarks
- **case (b)**: *"at C on the way from B to A"*
- **case (c)**: *"at intersection M, forward to A, left to B, right to D"* without message about the backward.

We assume that A, B, C, D, and M are named nodes in the navigation network. An important requirement is to avoid so-called too much information, which makes the user confused. For this reason, we do not include landmarks for **case (c)**. Similarly, it is recommended to include small number of landmark instruction for **case (a)** such like one for left and right each, for example *"a vending machine on the right and restroom on the left"*.

[4] http://handle.itu.int/11.1002/1000/13185, last accessed on 31 Dec. 2019.

5.2   Navigation Instruction

The second instruction type of INS for VIP is to provide turn-by-turn instructions for navigation. A set of navigation instructions is assigned to each *segment* of navigation network, which is defined as transition in IndoorGML. For each segment, the navigation instructions are given as the following order (we suppose that the user moves from p_1, and p_2, to p_3 in Fig. 3);

- **instruction 1 (starting instruction)** at p_1: e.g. *"go forward 10 steps"*,
- **instruction 2 (preparation instruction)** at p_2: e.g. *"5 steps before M"*, and
- **instruction 3 (turning instruction)** at p_3: e.g. *"turn right"*.

These three instructions are repeated for each segment except the following cases. The first exception is the case where the segment is too short to read all these instructions. In this case, we may skip instruction 2 or reduce them into one single instruction such as *"forward 4 steps and turn right"*. The second case is where the segment is too long that there is a long blank interval without any instruction between **instruction 1** and **instruction 2** during for example 15 s. In this case we insert an instruction for the current location (**case (a)**) defined in the previous Subsect. 5.1, such as *"on the way from A to M, a vending machine on the left, restroom on the right."*

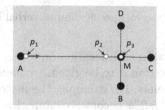

Fig. 3. Navigation instructions

5.3   Safety Instruction

The instructions about safety measures are of the first priority. It means that any safety instruction should be scheduled as the message of the first priority. For example *"slippery floor"* or *"stairs on the left"* belong to the safety instructions. They have to be given at the proper time and position without any delay.

5.4   Scheduling Instructions

Multiple instructions may be offered to VIP user during a limited time interval, which is determined by segment length and the speed of VIP user. Scheduling instructions is a critical functional requirement of INS for VIP, which are summarized as below;

- The instruction for the current location is activated when the VIP user presses the current location button on the smartphone application. It may start after the previous instruction or interrupt it upon the configuration. Note that the user has to stop when she/he listens the instructions on the current location. It means that the duration for this instruction do not need to be taken into account.
- The safety instruction should be scheduled as the first priority and overwrite any ongoing instructions.
- Given a set of instructions, we have to find the optimal schedule that satisfies their time interval specifications as shown in Fig. 4.

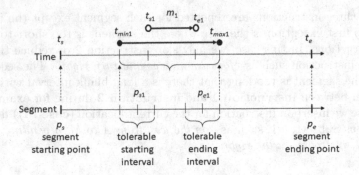

Fig. 4. Time interval specification of verbal instruction

There are mapping between each location on a segment and its passing time of the user. When an instruction is to be given, we have the meaningful interval with starting and ending points. For example, the instruction on landmark (e.g. *"vending machine on your left"*) becomes meaningless when the user goes too far from the vending machine. If we define the tolerable starting interval as e.g. 2 m, the message should start within $(-2\,\text{m}, 2\,\text{m})$. Accordingly we can find the tolerable time intervals for starting and ending points, which determine the total tolerable time interval (t_{min1}, t_{max1}) of a given message m_1 as shown in Fig. 4. At least the message m_1 should be given during this time interval and more strictly it should satisfy the time intervals for starting point and ending point.

We do not discuss the implementation issue of the instruction scheduling. Several approaches for real-time scheduling seem helpful to solve the instruction scheduling problem. We may classify the instruction types by their level of real-time constraints for example, safety real-time as the highest level, turning instruction as the next level, and landmarks as the lowest level. We leave this issue as a future work.

6   Conclusion

While several services of indoor navigation for visually impaired people have been developed, there are few work on the requirements analysis. Most of them are commercial products and their functional requirements are not explicitly specified. Although an outstanding work has been done to define a standard specification on INS for VIP, it is still abstract and does not specify technical details. In this work-in-progress paper, we define the technical specifications, which are focused on two aspects; indoor maps for VIP users and verbal instructions. The contributions of this paper are therefore first the specification of standard indoor maps for VIP, second, specification of verbal instruction generation, third, the instruction scheduling requirements.

We do not discuss the implementation issues but these requirements and specifications are to be reflected into a development project, VIM[5]. In this paper, it is assumed that the VIP users navigate in an relatively unknown area but it may be interesting to extend our work to VIP users navigating in a familiar environment and to partially sighted users as they may have different requirements.

References

1. Kulyukin, V., Gharpure, C., Nicholson, J., Pavithran, S.: RFID in robot-assisted indoor navigation for the visually impaired. In: 2004 IEEE/RSJ International Conference on Intelligent Robots and Systems (IROS) (IEEE Cat. No. 04CH37566), pp. 1979–1984. IEEE (2004)
2. Nakajima, M., Haruyama, S.: New indoor navigation system for visually impaired people using visible light communication. EURASIP J. Wireless Commun. Network. **2013**(1), 27 (2013)
3. Guerrero, L.A., Vasquez, F., Ochoa, S.F.: An indoor navigation system for the visually impaired. Sensors **12**(6), 8236–8258 (2012)
4. Ran, L., Helal, S., Moore, S.: Drishti: an integrated indoor/outdoor blind navigation system and service. In: Proceedings of the Second IEEE Annual Conference on Pervasive Computing and Communications 2004, pp. 23–30 (2004)
5. Yelamarthi, K., Haas, D., Nielsen, D., Mothersell, S.: RFID and GPS integrated navigation system for the visually impaired. In: Proceedings of 53rd IEEE International Midwest Symposium on Circuits and Systems 2010, pp. 1149–1152 (2010)
6. Chen, H.-E., Lin, Y.-Y., Chen, C.-H., Wang, I.: BlindNavi: a navigation app for the visually impaired smartphone user. In: Proceedings of the 33rd Annual ACM Conference Extended Abstracts on Human Factors in Computing Systems, pp. 19–24 (2015)
7. Kalia, A.A., Legge, G.E., Roy, R., Ogale, A.: Assessment of indoor route-finding technology for people who are visually impaired. J. Vis. Impairment Blindness **104**(3), 135–147 (2010)
8. Helal, A., Moore, S.E., Ramachandran, B.: Drishti: an integrated navigation system for visually impaired and disabled. In: Proceedings of the fifth IEEE International Symposium on Wearable Computers, pp. 149–156 (2001)
9. Gaunet, F., Briffault, X.: Exploring the functional specifications of a localized wayfinding verbal aid for blind pedestrians: simple and structured urban areas. Hum. Comput. Interact. **20**(3), 267–314 (2005)
10. Fryer, L., Freeman, J., Pring, L.: What verbal orientation information do blind and partially sighted people need to find their way around? A study of everyday

---

[5] the source code of prototype is available at https://github.com/STEMLab/VIM.

navigation strategies in people with impaired vision. Br. J. Vis. Impair. **31**(2), 123–138 (2013)

11. Brock, A.M., Truillet, P., Oriola, B., Picard, D., Jouffrais, C.: Interactivity improves usability of geographic maps for visually impaired people. Hum. Comput. Interact. **30**(2), 156–194 (2015)

12. Kulyukin, V.A., Nicholson, J., Ross, D.A., Marston, J.R., Gaunet, F.: The blind leading the blind: toward collaborative online route information management by individuals with visual impairments. In: Proceedings of AAAI Spring Symposium: Social Information Processing 2008, pp. 54–59 (2008)

13. Clark-Carter, D.D., Heyes, A.D., Howarth, C.I.: The efficiency and walking speed of visually impaired people. Ergonomics **29**(6), 779–789 (1986)

14. Li, K.J., Zlatanova, S., Torres-Sospedra, J., Perez-Navarro, A., Laoudias, C., Moreira, A.: Survey on indoor map standards and formats. In: Proceedings of 2019 International Conference on Indoor Positioning and Indoor Navigation (IPIN), pp. 1–8. IEEE (2019)

15. Lee, J.Y., Li, K.J., Zlatanova, S., Kolbe, T.H., Nagel, C., Becker, T.: OGC IndoorGML, Open Geospatial Consortium standard 14–005r5 (2014)

16. Kang, H.K., Li, K.J.: A standard indoor spatial data model-OGC IndoorGML and implementation approaches. ISPRS Int. J. Geo Inf. **6**(4), 116 (2017)

Simulating COVID-19 Spreads in Indoor Space

Arman Assankhanov and Ki-Joune Li[✉]

Department of Computer Science and Engineering, Pusan National University, Pusan
46241, South Korea
{arman,lik}@pnu.edu
http://lik.pnu.edu

Abstract. It is known that the transmissibility of COVID-19 is higher
in indoor space than outdoor. The fact that the indoor space is usually
closed and has less factors to take into account than outdoor may facilitate the analysis of COVID-19 infection. However, few works have been
done on the analysis on COVID-19 transmissibility in indoor space. In
this paper, we discuss simulation methods to analyze the transmissibility
in indoor space, particularly a simulation environment consisting of three
components; indoor maps, positions and trajectories of persons in indoor
space, and infection models of COVID-19 in indoor space. And we analyze the requirements and design issues of each component. Among three
COVID-19 infection models, we developed a simulation tool for indoor
person-person infection model. While only the person-person infection
model has been implemented for the simulation, the other two models of
COVID-19 are planned to be designed and implemented in the future.

Keywords: COVID-19 spread simulation · Indoor maps · Indoor
trajectories · InCOVID

1 Introduction

The transmissibility of COVID-19 is strong in indoor space, especially where
space is closed and of high density of people [1]. In order to respond to the spread
of COVID-19 in indoor space, we need to analyze the properties of indoor space,
which are quite different from outdoor. For example, an indoor space is parti-
tioned into a set of cells such as rooms and corridors and they are connected via
doors, stairs, and lifts. The navigation of persons between rooms in indoor space
happens always through these connections [19]. While the infection probability
is mainly determined by the distance, the distance is not always determined by
Euclidean distance. For example if two persons are in other rooms, then the
infection probability becomes zero even though the Euclidean distance is small.

This work was supported by BK21PLUS, Creative Human Resource Development Program for IT Convergence and grant(21NSIP-B135746-05) from National Spatial Information Research Program (NSIP) funded by Ministry of Land, Infrastructure and
Transport of Korean government.

F. Karimipour and S. Storandt (Eds.): W2GIS 2022, LNCS 13238, pp. 131–140, 2022.
https://doi.org/10.1007/978-3-031-06245-2_12

In our work, we discuss the transmissibility of COVID-19 in indoor space. Not only the positions and trajectories of people but also the indoor properties such as indoor structures are taken into account for our work. The analysis of COVID-19 could be ideally conducted with real data sets collected from the indoor spaces where spreads of the virus had already taken place. However, these real data sets are difficult to collect due to privacy issue and limited to cover sufficiently the whole cases of the analysis. For example, when we analyze the vulnerability of COVID-19 spread in a given indoor space, we could not conduct it before it would really happen. For this reason, we discuss simulation methods for COVID-19 spread in indoor space by using given indoor map and generating synthetic trajectories of persons in the given indoor space. The simulation method discussed in the paper is mainly composed of three parts; trajectories of people, COVID-19 infection models, and indoor maps.

The generation of synthetic trajectories is a crucial function of the simulation as it determines the position of each person at each second and allows to compute the distance between people. It means that the synthetic trajectories should be similar with real ones. Several factors such as user profile, the nature of indoor space, and the function of cell are helpful in generating realistic trajectories. In a shopping mall, for example, different movement patterns may be applied depending on user profile about whether she/he is an employee of store or visitor. In college campus building, they may be either faculties, students, or staffs, where faculties and students enter into a classroom and stay there during one hour while staffs work in office room. We can generate the trajectories according to this profile.

The COVID-19 infection models are classified into three types; person-person model, person-space model, and person-object, where each of the infection models requires different data and functionalities. Indoor maps are essential in not only generating indoor trajectories but also applying each COVID-19 infection model.

In this paper, we will discuss the requirements of COVID-19 simulation tool and design issues. The requirements for each of three infection models will be analyzed in terms of indoor spatial data and functionalities. In particular, we focus on the first infection model, that is the person-person model, and present a prototype implementation of the simulation method called InCOVID. In order to validate its feasibility, we will show the result of experiment, which was conducted with a real indoor space data. The rest of this paper is organized as follows; in Sect. 2, we survey the related works on the analysis of COVID-19 in indoor space. In Sect. 3, we discuss the requirements of the simulation methods. The prototype developed for person-person infection model is presented in Sect. 4 with its experiment with a real building and the conclusion is given in Sect. 5.

2   Related Works and Motivations

In several studies, it has been reported that the COVID-19 infections mostly happen in indoor space [1, 2]. Several factors affect the transmissibility of COVID-19, among which the distance between infected and uninfected persons is of most important one. Unlike outdoor space, there are other factors, such as indoor structures and mobility of persons, affecting the transmissibility beside the distance itself. Park et al. [3] reported that the spread of coronavirus at the call center in South Korea, March 2020, took place in lobby and lifts. It means that indoor structures such as lobby, stairs, lifts, and hallways have to be considered in the analysis of COVID-19 spread.

In general, the infection models of COVID-19 are classified into three types [13,14] as follows;

- **person-person model**: infection by droplets ($\geq 5\,\mu$m) between an infected person and uninfected person,
- **person-place**: infection via airbone ($\leq 5\,\mu$m5) [4], where *place* means the space where infected person left the virus such as a room,
- **person-surface**: indirect infection by object surfaces such as door handles

Note that place and surface of the classification above means While our work aims to analyze the indoor spread of COVID-19 by these models, we focus on the first infection model (person-person). As our first step, we aim to develop the simulation model for the infection of COVID-19 via droplets to nearby persons [15]. The second and third infection models would be excluded from the first step of our work as the details of these infection models are not fully discovered. They would be included in our work of next steps.

Few works have been done for the analysis of indoor spread of COVID-19 virus, while some applications have been developed and used to track the infections of COVID-19 in indoor and outdoor spaces. Tracking applications such as TraceTogether in Singapore [16], CovidSafe in Australia [17], and [18] in USA are mostly limited to outdoor space. They do not consider any indoor structures or movement patters in indoor space. In [19], an interesting study was presented to track the infections by three infection models in indoor space. They proposed a method for tracking the infection by using the arrival and departure times of cell space and OGC IndoorGML, which is a standard of indoor spatial information. [10,12].

While previous works have focused on tracking the infection in indoor or outdoor spaces, no work has been done for analyzing how indoor structures would affect the transmissibility of coronavirus. This analysis would allow to discover the weak points of COVID-19 spread of a given building and eventually find preventive measures for minimizing the transmissibility. We therefore aim to develop analysis methods of COVID-19 spread in indoor space.

3   Requirements for the Analysis on Indoor COVID-19 Spread

The analysis of indoor COVID-19 spread consists of three components as below;

- **infection model**: In order to conduct the analysis, a infection model has to be determined among person-person, person-space, and person-surface models as different data sets are required accordingly.
- **indoor maps**: Indoor structures significantly affect the transmissibility. For example, sharing a single lift of a building by all inhabitants may significantly increase the transimissibility of COVID-19, while we may lower the transmissibity by partitioning a work space into small office rooms for each staff. Indoor maps are therefore a fundamental requirement for the analysis.
- **positions and trajectories of persons**: The location of person is also one of main factors determining the distance between persons and therefore the infectivity. We need the trajectories of inhabitants determining the locations of each person at each time. The collection of the trajectories is crucial in analyzing the COVID-19 spread in indoor space.

3.1 Indoor Maps

Each type of infection models requires different indoor spatial information. First, staying in the same room with an infected person increases the transmissibility by the person-person model. The room geometry is necessary to determine whether or not they stay in the same room. Second, as the virus spread via airbone according to the person-place model, we need to analyze the airflow in indoor space and indoor CFD (Computational Fluid Dynamics) is useful in the analysis. Several types of indoor spatial information are needed to analyze the airflow, including 3D geometry of rooms, windows, doors, locations of big furniture and installations, and ventilation facilities affecting airflow. Third, the person-surface model requires the information about indoor features such as door handles, handrails, and lift buttons that can be touched by infected and uninfected persons. These requirements about indoor maps are summarized in Table 1.

Table 1. Indoor spatial data requirements for three infection models

Infection model	Dimension	Indoor data requirements
Person-person model	2D	Cell boundary
Person-place model	3D	Cell boundary, doors, windows,big objects, and ventilation facilities
Person-surface model	2D	Cell boundary, surfaces of objects

3.2 Positions and Trajectories of Persons

Next to indoor maps, positions of each person in indoor space need to be prepared for the analysis of COVID-19 spread. Ideally real position data sets of each person could be collected for the analysis but it is difficult to collect sufficient and diverse position data sets due to the privacy issue. A more practical approach is rather to generate virtual trajectories in a given indoor space as long as the synthetic trajectories are similar with real ones. In our work, we adopt the generation of synthetic trajectories in a given indoor space.

In order to generate realistic trajectories, several factors need to be taken into account. First, we need indoor navigation networks of given indoor space, which can be derived from indoor maps and may vary according to time, transportation modes, and types of disability. Second, different patterns of mobility should be applied depending on user profile. Employees working at a shop in shopping mall, enter into the building via a gate, go to their shop and stay there for their working time. However, visitors go around in the shopping mall after they enter into the building for shorter time, i.e. one hour. In a campus building, students may stay in a classroom for a hour and move to other classrooms, while staffs work in their office room during the working time. All these factors may be parameterized in the trajectory generation tool.

Several generation tools have been developed so far such as IndoorSTG [22], Vita [23], and SIMOGEN [24]. In our work, we used SIMOGEN for its flexibility with several parameters mentioned above.

3.3   Infection Models of COVID-19

Given indoor maps and trajectories in a given indoor space, we apply infection models of COVID-19 to determine whether an infection happened or not. We simply define it as an infection function F_I as

$$F_I(M, p, q, t) = b \tag{1}$$

where M is indoor map, p and q are trajectories of infected and uninfected persons, t is a timestamp, and $b \in \{\texttt{true}, \texttt{false}\}$.

This infection function can be separated into three functions $F_{p2person}$, $F_{p2place}$, and $F_{p2surface}$ according to the infection model, while F_I is defined as a conjunctive form of three functions;

$$F_I(M, p, q, t) = (F_{p2person} \vee F_{p2place} \vee F_{p2surface})(M, p, q, t). \tag{2}$$

It means that the infection happens if any of these infection function return true. Let us discuss each of these infection models.

Person-Person Infection Model: This is the simplest one among three infection models. As we assume that the COVID-19 is infected by droplets bigger than 5 µm, the distance between infected and uninfected persons is critical. The probability of infection $p(a, b)$ by this model is defined as below;

$$p(a, b) = \begin{cases} 0 & \text{if } a \in C_a, b \in C_b, \text{ where } C_a \neq C_b \\ p_d & \text{if } a, b \in C, \ d(a, b) < d_0 \\ p_d(\frac{d_0}{d(a,b)})^2 & \text{if } a, b \in C, \ d(a, b) \geq d_0 \end{cases} \tag{3}$$

where a and b are an infected and uninfected persons, C_a and C_b are the rooms where they are staying respectively, $d(a, b)$ is the distance between a and b, and p_d is the infection probability when they are at the threshold distance d_0 between them. The basic idea of this model is explained by Fig. 1. When an infected person a and uninfected person b_1 are in the same room C_1 and the distance between them d_1 is lower than a threshold d_0, the infection probability is p_d. When they are in the same room but $d_1 \geq d_0$, the probability of infection is proportional to the inverse of the their distance square. If they stay in different rooms (a and b_2), the infection probability becomes 0. We expect that more accurate models would be replaced with more considerations.

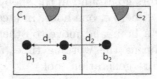

Fig. 1. Person-person infection model

Person-Place Infection Model: Several cases of airbone infection are reported. It is recommended to reduce air circulation and install HVAC for the ventilation of fresh air into the building. In order to analyze the person-place infection model, we first need the airflow analysis in indoor space. It is expected that CFD tools would be helpful to analyze the airflow considering ventilation and HVAC facilities as well as doors, windows, and big furniture and installations [5, 6, 20, 21]. It means the airflow analysis requires the geometries of these objects and features in indoor space. Second, we have to track the arrival and departure times of infected persons to each cell including room, lift, hallway, and lobby. As reported by [7], the coronavirus stays alive during three hours in the air. It means that we need to track the rooms and airflow containing the coronavirus. For example, the persons visiting within three hours at the same room where any infected person stayed or coronavirus virus is supposed to circulate, would be suspected to be infected. It is also expected that the longer we stay at the place where the air contains the virus, the higher is the infection probability. However, it is difficult to consider all these conditions together including the arrival and departure times of infected and non infected persons as well as the indoor airflow and ventilation by HVAC. Unfortunately no integral method for the infection analysis of this model is available so far.

Person-Surface Infection Model: The third model refers to the case where the infection happens by touching the surface of the same object such as door handles, lift buttons, or handrails [8]. The survival time of coronavirus differs depending on the materials; 4 h for cooper, 24 h for cardboard, and 72 h for plastic and steel [9]. In order to analyze the spread of COVID-19, we need to find the objects that the infected person may touch and examine the trajectories of uninfected persons whether they come across with the surface of the objects during 72 h.

4   In COVID- A Simulation Tool for Person-Person COVID-19 Infection Model

4.1   Design and Implementation of InCOVID

In this section, we present InCOVID that we developed as an open source software[1] to analyze the COVID-19 spread by simulation. The process of InCOVID is summarized in Fig. 2.

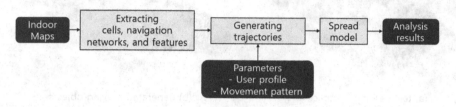

Fig. 2. Process overview on InCOVID

The first input to InCOVID is indoor maps of a given building. As discussed in Sect. 3.1, person-person model requires the geometries and properties of cells, and navigation networks. We extract them from indoor maps in OGC IndoorGML, which is an OGC standard for indoor maps and provides richer semantics as well as geometries of indoor space than other indoor map formats [11]. This standard satisfies the requirements discussed in Sect. 3.1.

After extracting the necessary data from indoor maps, we also receive additional inputs of the parameters for generating trajectories. It contains several parameters including the number of persons, profile of each person, arrival and departure times, and movement patterns, which allow to generate realistic trajectories. We improved an existing open source tool, called SIMOGEN (Synthetic Indoor MOving objects GENerator)[2] for indoor trajectory generation [24]. As the final step of InCOVID, the person-person infection model is applied using the trajectories and the cell geometries extracted from indoor maps. We determine whether uninfected persons are in a same cell of any infected person and approximate the infection probability by the distance between infected and uninfected persons. We also discover the locations where the infections are supposed to take place for computing the hot spot zones of the infections. Actually these hot spots can be considered as week points of given building where proper preventive measures are required.

4.2   Experiment

In order to validate the feasibility of InCOVID, we conducted an experiment with a real building, a big shopping complex in Seoul. The numbers of rooms,

---

[1] https://github.com/STEMLab/InCOVID.
[2] https://github.com/STEMLab/SIMOGEN.

entrances, floors, and stairs or lifts are 2,162, 8, 17, and 208 respectively and the left side of Fig. 3 shows this indoor space. The parameter values for generating trajectories are summarized in Table 2.

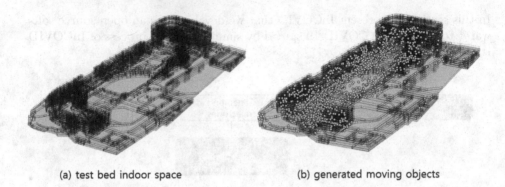

(a) test bed indoor space   (b) generated moving objects

Fig. 3. Test site

Table 2. Parameter settings for trajectory generation

Parameters	Descriptions	Values
n	Number of persons	1000, 5000
r_s	Ratio of stationary persons (employees)	0.1, 0.2, 0.3, 0.4, 0.5
Staying	Arrival and	- employee: 9 am to 8 pm
Interval	Departure time	- visitors: one hour between 9 am and 8 pm

The threshold distance for infection and incubation period are set to 2m and two days, respectively. We set the simulation tool to stop when the ratio of infected persons arrives to 90%, And we assume that the same persons enters to this building for each day. A part of simulation results is shown in Fig. 4. It is only an example of the simulation results and unfortunately we do not have any real data sets that we could compare with our simulation results so far. We expect that benchmark data sets would be available and could be used to validate this simulation tool.

5   Conclusion

The transmissibility of COVID-19 is higher than other epidemic diseases and particularly, stronger in indoor space than outdoor. In this work-in progress paper, we discussed several topics of COVID-19 spread analysis in indoor space and the requirements of three infection models - person-person model, person-place model, and person-surface model - were presented. InCOVID, a prototype

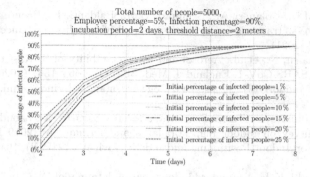

Fig. 4. Simulation with different ratios of initially infected persons

simulation tool for analyzing person-person infection model, was shown and an experiment with real indoor space was presented to validate its feasibility.

Future work will include three parts. First the simulation tool will include the remaining infection models, person-place and person-surface models. Second the trajectory generation tool will be improved to produce more realistic cases. We expect that deep learning approaches such as GAN (Generative Adversarial Network) would be helpful to generate more realistic trajectories. It may be also interesting to compare the synthetic data from this tool and real trajectories if it would be available. Third, the validation of this model and tool is to be included in the future work. We expect any benchmark test data set would be available in the future. We may also consider temporal properties of indoor space such as accessibility of doors depending on time. It may be considered for the improvement of SIMOGEN.

References

1. Morawska, L., et al.: How can airborne transmission of COVID-19 indoors be minimised? Environ. Int. **142**, 105832–105839 (2020)
2. Du, W., Wang, G.: Indoor air pollution was nonnegligible during covid-19 lockdown. Aerosol Air Qual. Res. **20**(9), 1851–1855 (2020)
3. Park, S.Y., et al.: Coronavirus disease outbreak in call center. South Korea. Emerg. infect. Dis. **26**(8), 1666 (2020)
4. Bhagat, R.K., Wykes, M.D., Dalziel, S.B., Linden, P.F.: Effects of ventilation on the indoor spread of COVID-19. J. Fluid Mech. **903** (2020)
5. Zhao, B., Li, X., Yan, Q.: A simplified system for indoor airflow simulation. Build. Environ. **38**(4), 543–552 (2003)
6. Yang, L., Ye, M.: CFD simulation research on residential indoor air quality. Sci. Total Environ. **472**, 1137–1144 (2014)
7. Aboubakr, H.A., Sharafeldin, T.A., Goyal, S.M.: Stability of SARS-CoV-2 and other corona viruses in the environment and on common touch surfaces and the influence of climatic conditions. A Rev. Transboundary Emerg. Dis. **68**(2), 296–312 (2021)

8. Mondelli, M.U., Colaneri, M., Seminari, E.M., Baldanti, F., Bruno, R.: Low risk of SARS-CoV-2 transmission by fomites in real-life conditions. Lancet. Infect. Dis **21**(5), e112 (2021)
9. Van Doremalen, N., et al.: Aerosol and surface stability of SARS-CoV-2 as compared with SARS-CoV-1. England J. Med. **382**(16), 1564–1567 (2020)
10. OGC, OGC IndoorGML. https://www.ogc.org/standards/indoorgml. Accessed 19 Jan 2021
11. Li, K.J., Zlatanova, S., Torres-Sospedra, J., Pérez-Navarro, A., Laoudias, C., Moreira, A.: Survey on indoor map standards and formats. In: 2019 International Conference on Indoor Positioning and Indoor Navigation (IPIN), Pisa, 1–8. IEEE (2019)
12. Kang, H.K., Li, K.J.: A standard indoor spatial data model-OGC IndoorGML and implementation approaches. ISPRS Int. J. Geo-Inf. **64**, 116 (2017)
13. The Lancet Respiratory Medicine Editorial: COVID-19 transmission-up in the air. Lancet. Infect. Dis **812**, 1159 (2020)
14. World health organization: coronavirus disease (COVID-19): how is it transmitted. https://www.who.int/news-room/q-a-detail/coronavirus-disease-covid-19-how-is-it-transmitted. Accessed 18 Jan 2021
15. Riemer, K., Ciriello, R., Peter, S., Schlagwein, D.: Digital contact-tracing adoption in the COVID-19 pandemic: IT governance for collective action at the societal level. Eur. J. Inf. Syst. **296**, 731–745 (2020)
16. OpenTrace. https://github.com/opentrace-community. Accessed 19 Jan 2021
17. CovidSafe. https://github.com/AU-COVIDSafe. Accessed 19 Jan 2021
18. PACT. East Coast. https://pact.mit.edu/. Accessed 20 Jan 2021
19. Ojagh, S., Saeedi, S., Liang, S.H.: A person-to-person and person-to-place COVID-19 contact tracing system based on OGC IndoorGML. ISPRS Int. J. Geo-Inf. **10**(1), 2–35 (2021)
20. Chen, Q., Srebric, J.: A procedure for verification, validation, and reporting of indoor environment CFD analyses. HVAC R Res. **8**(2), 201–216 (2002)
21. Gilani, S., Montazeri, H., Blocken, B.: CFD simulation of stratified indoor environment in displacement ventilation: validation and sensitivity analysis. Build. Environ. **95**, 299–313 (2016)
22. Huang, C., Jin, P., Wang, H., Wang, N., Wan, S., Yue, L.: IndoorSTG: a extensible tool to generate trajectory data for indoor moving objects, In: IEEE 14th International Conference on Mobile Data Management, IEEE Computer Society, Milan, pp. 341–343 (2013)
23. Li, H., Lu, H., Chen, X., Chen, G., Chen, K., Shou, L.: VITA: a versatile toolkit for generating indoor mobility data for real-world buildings. In: VLDB 2016 Conference, VLDB endowment, New Delhi, India, pp. 1453–1456 (2016)
24. Ryoo, H.G., Kim, S.J., Li, K.J.: Synthetic trajectory generation tool for indoor moving objects. J. Korean Soc. Geospatial Inf. Syst. **24**(4), 59–66 (2016)

Comparison of Indoor Positioning Methods Based on AR Visual and WiFi Fingerprinting Method

Yijun He[1] and Xiang Li[1,2(✉)]

[1] Key Laboratory of Geographic Information Science (Ministry of Education) and School of Geographic Sciences, East China Normal University, Shanghai 200241, China
xli@geo.ecnu.edu.cn

[2] Shanghai Key Lab for Urban Ecological Processes and Eco-Restoration, East China Normal University, Shanghai 200241, China

Abstract. Location-based service (LBS) has become an indispensable part of our daily life. However, indoor positioning system at early stage is not able to meet the urgent need for indoor LBS. Low-cost indoor positioning technology without additional equipment is the current challenge in LBS field. In this paper, two typical indoor positioning methods are selected: AR (Augmented Reality) based visual positioning method and WiFi based positioning method. Experiments are conducted to compare the two indoor positioning methods from multiple perspectives. Results show that performance of the two methods are similar in the aspects such as positioning time consumption, equipment cost, usability and difficulty level during preprocessing. Main differences between them are as follows: AR visual positioning method is more accurate and stable, with its mean average error at around 0.85 m and max error at 3.18 m. It's suitable for indoor environment rich in texture and stable in light. WiFi positioning has high values in error related variables. Its MAE is about 3 m and more volatile with extreme values. However, it has an edge in usability including power consumption indicator. It's more efficient in data acquisition stage and is suitable for large-scale positioning. This paper tends to provide reference for selection of indoor positioning methods.

Keywords: Comparison of indoor positioning methods · AR visual positioning · WiFi fingerprint indoor positioning · Indoor positioning and navigation

1 Introduction

With popularization of intelligent mobile devices and continuous improvement of their sensor configurations, it is becoming more and more common to obtain users' real-time location and location-based Service (LBS) by means of mobile devices [1]. Due to multipath effect of signal caused by blocking of walls, satellite signal intensity is greatly weakened indoors. Thus, the mature outdoor positioning technology cannot be directly applied to indoor positioning. Therefore, study on indoor positioning method has been the focus of indoor LBS, among which, it is a major difficulty how to achieve low-cost and large-scale indoor positioning without additional equipment [2, 3].

© Springer Nature Switzerland AG 2022
F. Karimipour and S. Storandt (Eds.): W2GIS 2022, LNCS 13238, pp. 141–151, 2022.
https://doi.org/10.1007/978-3-031-06245-2_13

Most current indoor positioning technologies are limited by site conditions or dependent on additional equipment [5]. Geomagnetic positioning and inertial navigation positioning method needs user's mobile device only, but the stability and accuracy cannot meet the requirements of small-scale indoor scene [6]. Positioning methods based on Radio Frequency, Infrared, Ultra wide-band and etc. require external equipment layout in the environment [5]. WiFi signals are the existing external signal sources covering most of today's indoor environments, without additional deployment costs, which makes WiFi-based positioning a mainstream method [2]. Visual positioning technology takes the camera of users' portable device as sensor and extracts features using computer vision to match images with location. As it has the advantages of low cost and fine scale, it has attracted wide attention [4, 8].

Among positioning methods based on WiFi, the fingerprint positioning technology based on Received Signal Strength (RSS) is relatively typical [9, 12]. Classical positioning systems based on WiFi location fingerprint include RADAR system [10], Horus system, etc. [11]. RSS values are obtained through repeated frame listening and response between mobile terminal devices and surrounding wireless Access Points (AP). With no need for specific location of AP, the method is relatively convenient in signal data acquisition and low in cost, however susceptible to ambient interference [12].

Driven by development of computer vision, visual positioning methods based on image matching have gained popularity. An image retrieval technology called BoW (Bag of Words) was raised at the International Computer Vision Conference [13]. Lowe [14] proposed a local feature matching method, SIFT (Scale-invariant Feature Transform), and Bay et al. [15] subsequently proposed SURF (Speeded Up Robust Features), which are insusceptible for changes in perspective, scaling and illumination. Researchers realized positioning and navigation systems using methods above [16, 17].

Combination of Augmented Reality (AR) with traditional image vision technology [4, 26] expands the breadth and depth of related applications [18]. With real-time positioning and map construction framework, inertial measurement and artificial intelligence as supporting technologies [20], AR assisted indoor positioning and navigation naturally become an essential part of LBS and AR services [7, 19].

As an emerging indoor positioning technology [2, 8], AR visual positioning needs to be compared with other indoor positioning methods for comprehensive evaluation. Most studies simply use positioning error to evaluate the quality of positioning methods [23, 24]. In addition to error indicators, positioning time, method extensibility (locatable range and number of users, etc.), algorithm complexity, robustness and cost are important quantitative indicators [9, 12, 25]. Qualitative factors such as the ability to resist environmental interference, the need for sample data and deployment of auxiliary equipment can also be included to measure positioning algorithms [26].

Based on existing studies, this paper selects two typical methods of Wi-Fi positioning and AR visual positioning for evaluation and comparison. An indoor positioning and navigation system is accomplished on Unity platform using these two indoor positioning methods separately. Wi-Fi positioning module adopts the fingerprint positioning method based on RSS and applies KNN for location matching and Kalman filter for signal processing. Experiments are then carried out and a quality evaluation system is established. The advantages and disadvantages of the two indoor positioning methods are compared from multiple perspectives, providing reference for related research and selection of indoor positioning methods.

2   Related Positioning Methods

2.1   AR Visual Positioning Method

AR visual positioning method is based on computer vision technology with image match-ing as the core. Feature points with location that can describe the environment will be extracted from images to build 3D feature point cloud database. By matching the local feature point cloud extracted from real-time scene and global feature point cloud in database, users' position and orientation can be obtained [20–22] (Fig. 1).

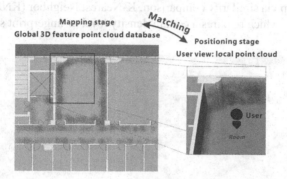

Fig. 1. Schematic diagram of positioning based on sparse spatial map

AR visual positioning can be realized by two stages: mapping and positioning. At the mapping stage, developers need to scan the study area with handheld devices to construct 3D feature point cloud, namely sparse spatial maps. Firstly, SIFT is used to extract feature points. Secondly, these features are quantified in the feature space by clustering algorithm. Each image tile is marked with the nearest clustering label (visual vocabulary), and the word bag model composed of visual words is trained to extract the 2D feature points. In the process of user movement, the image frames with the highest similarity are selected for feature matching. Finally, through image feature matching and multi-view forward intersection measurement, the 3D feature points cloud database is built to quantify the study scenario [18, 21]. At the positioning stage, after the pre-constructed sparse spatial map is localized, the user needs to open the camera so as to construct current 3D feature points around the user. Via feature point cloud matching, it's then able to locate the user in real time. The study selects EasyAR, a domestic Augmented Reality engine, to accomplish the AR visual positioning module [27].

2.2   Wi-Fi Positioning Method

Wi-Fi location methods can be mainly divided into three categories: geometric mea-surement method, approximation method and scene analysis method [9]. The fingerprint positioning method based on Wi-Fi belongs to the scene analysis method, in which RSS is generally selected as the signal feature to describe the environment. According to IEEE802.11 protocol, users' terminal can scan all the channels and send Probe Request frame to all the APs for acquisition of MAC address and RSS [28]. As long as the WiFi function of the user's device is turned on, it's feasible to calculate user's location.

The RSS fingerprint positioning algorithm can be divided into mapping stage and positioning stage as well (Fig. 2). At the mapping stage, developers collect RSS fingerprint in the study area with 0.5 m apart. By collecting coordinates, MAC address for each AP and RSS value of each sample, a position-based fingerprint map is built covering the scenario. The signal obtained needs to be preprocessed to approximate real user trajectory by filtering RSS values with large skewness and small probability. Kalman Filter, a kind of state estimation algorithm, is applied to smooth the signal [29]. At the positioning stage, the RSS fingerprint of the user's actual location will be matched with the fingerprint map via similarity comparison. K-Nearest Neighbor (KNN) is applied to location matching, which requires a certain density level of fingerprint samples.

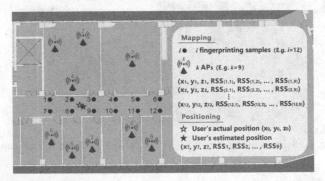

Fig. 2. Schematic diagram of fingerprint indoor positioning based on WiFi

2.3 Accuracy Evaluation System of Positioning Method

The index system for evaluating and comparing indoor positioning methods is shown in the following Table 1:

Table 1. Variable design of the quality measurement of positioning methods.

Indicator type	Specific indicators	Traits to measure
Error	MAE	Overall accuracy of algorithm (core)
	Extreme error	Range of fluctuations in positioning
	SDE	Stability of algorithm
	Cumulative distribution function of the distance errors (CDF)	Overall precision of algorithm

(continued)

Table 1. (*continued*)

Indicator type	Specific indicators	Traits to measure
Usability	Positioning time	Positioning timeliness (core)
	Power consumption	Power consumption of algorithm
	System size	Portability of algorithms
Extensibility	Additional equipment cost	Extensibility of the algorithm (core)
	Mapping time per unit area	Applicability of algorithm
Robustness	Error change under light interference	Ability to resist environmental interference
	Error change under electronic interference	Ability to resist environmental interference
Subjective judgement	Difficulty of development	Algorithm selection from developers' view
	Complexity of preprocessing	Algorithm selection from developers' view
	Applicable site area	Application scenarios of the algorithm

3 Experiment

3.1 Experimental Area

This study selected the 6th and 7th floors of an office building on a campus as the experimental area. Each floor covers about $1718\ m^2$ and the corridor is around $162.36\ m^2$. The room where the first experiment in Sect. 3.2 is conducted covers $80.64\ m^2$. The 3D diagram of the study area is shown in Fig. 3. The indoor positioning and navigation system used in the experiment was developed using C# on Unity2019 platform. The APK was tested on the Xiaomi 10 Ultra edition mobile phone on Android system.

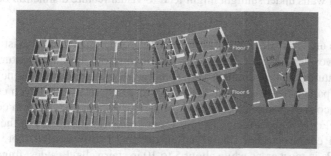

Fig. 3. 3D model of the building in the experiment

3.2 Experimental Results and Analysis

Experiments on Positioning in Room and Corridor. The overall positioning accuracy and stability of WiFi positioning in the room are lower than that in the corridor. Due to the small scope of the room, the difference within RSS fingerprint is small, and thus there exist drift phenomenon in location estimation. Besides, WiFi positioning may be interfered by electronic devices in the room. AR visual positioning indicates a better result in room than in corridor. In view of the nature of visual positioning, rich texture features in the room make the feature map construction faster and less prone to tracking errors (Fig. 4). The initial positioning takes less than 1 s, and MAE is about 0.45 m.

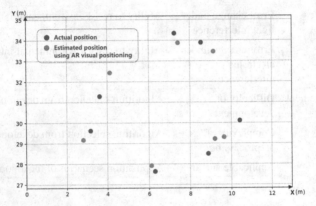

Fig. 4. Verification dot distribution inside the room based on AR visual positioning

Experiments on Positioning During the Day and at Night. AR visual positioning is greatly affected by ambient light. When 3D point cloud data is collected at night, it is difficult to capture detailed features. As there are limited number of 3D feature points collected, location tracking sometimes goes wrong during map construction. In another case, if sparse spatial map constructed at night is used for daytime positioning, it sometimes occurred apparent offsets in anchor points. The possible reason is that reflective objects and texture of walls under sunlight might lead to visual feature distinction between day and night.

Experiments on Multi-floor Positioning. In this experiment, there exist drawbacks using both two methods. For AR visual positioning, due to single texture of stairs, number of feature points are limited. Map constructed in stairwells are prone to separate or shift from parts to parts. For instance, if the topology relation between corridor and stairwell is incorrect, positioning might go wrong when a user steps from corridor into the stairwell. For WiFi positioning, staircases are rather far from APs in the rooms and hence, few AP can be detected. Using GetSensorData2.1 software [30], there are over 20 detectable APs in most areas while about 5 to 10 in stairwells. Besides, fingerprint data in the same horizontal area on the 6th floor and 7th floor are vertically close to each other. They could be mistakenly determined as adjacent fingerprint nodes by KNN location matching method. Therefore, 3D positioning system cannot directly copy the common 2D localization pattern and perhaps floors need to be determined in advance.

Overall Positioning Experiment

In order to compare WiFi positioning and AR visual positioning in a more comprehensive way, 23 verification points were selected in this experiment, and coordinate sampling was carried out during localization using the two methods. The experiment was conducted during daytime under good light condition. The verification results are shown in Table 2, and the distribution of verification points is shown in Fig. 5.

Table 2. Verification of indoor positioning results.

Verification points	Actual coordinates		Estimated coordinates using AR visual positioning		Miss distance (m)	Estimated coordinates using WiFi positioning		Miss distance (m)
	X	Y	X	Y		X	Y	
1	0.062	2.087	0.027	1.778	**0.310**	0.477	0.237	**1.896**
2	−1.568	0.577	−1.592	0.511	**0.070**	−1.546	0.067	**0.510**
3	1.524	0.620	1.598	0.315	**0.314**	1.258	0.022	**0.655**
4	−4.750	1.056	−4.305	1.021	**0.446**	−2.247	1.227	**2.509**
5	−6.973	0.356	−6.493	0.347	**0.480**	−1.785	1.498	**5.313**
6	−6.883	2.701	−6.466	2.685	**0.417**	−5.601	2.671	**1.282**
7	−7.024	4.746	−6.846	4.202	**0.573**	−5.521	6.739	**2.496**
8	−6.864	6.140	−6.570	6.440	**0.420**	−5.955	4.907	**1.533**
9	−5.909	13.003	−5.398	12.735	**0.577**	−3.707	10.872	**3.064**
10	−5.058	14.371	−4.996	14.107	**0.271**	−4.549	12.136	**2.292**
11	−4.438	16.739	−4.809	16.521	**0.431**	−4.015	15.442	**1.364**
12	−4.044	16.846	−4.320	17.505	**0.715**	−3.231	17.698	**1.178**
13	−2.970	19.830	−1.632	21.847	**2.420**	−2.612	21.850	**2.052**
14	−2.199	23.315	−1.973	24.041	**0.761**	−4.049	12.136	**11.330**
15	−0.798	25.315	−0.175	26.488	**1.328**	−3.393	13.940	**11.667**
16	−0.218	24.161	−0.096	24.955	**0.803**	0.720	26.338	**2.371**
17	−0.787	26.856	0.976	27.585	**1.907**	−1.632	23.812	**3.159**
18	−0.021	30.102	−0.175	30.488	**0.415**	−0.071	27.433	**2.669**
19	1.685	33.693	0.976	33.585	**0.717**	−0.793	33.286	**2.510**
20	4.682	42.076	4.045	38.965	**3.175**	6.198	47.329	**5.468**
21	6.097	48.411	5.783	48.358	**0.319**	6.198	47.329	**1.086**
22	6.646	46.784	7.503	47.119	**0.920**	6.835	48.052	**1.282**
23	6.559	50.789	8.418	50.720	**1.860**	6.081	48.804	**2.041**

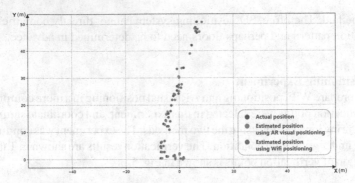

Fig. 5. Verification dot distribution of AR visual positioning and positioning based on WiFi

The experimental results indicate that the positioning results of the two methods have the following characteristics: (1) The drift position using WiFi positioning is within the spatial range of data pre-collection, while some biased points using AR method could "pass through the wall". (2) The 20th and the 21th verification point have coincident estimated coordinates. On noticing both of them lies in the end of a corridor, with sparse data collection, the sampling density on the edge of scenes should be increased. (3) According to the distribution diagram of verification points in the experiment (Fig. 5), as the range of 0–10 m on Y-axis is close to lift lobby with rich texture features, the predicted locations using AR method in this region almost coincide with true locations, while in the middle section of corridor, the accuracy is lower due to lots of repeated textures. Therefore, AR visual positioning method suits for relatively fixed areas with rich and unique features, avoiding areas with repeated doors and white walls.

Table 3. Comparison between AR visual positioning and Wi-Fi fingerprint indoor positioning.

Indicator types	Specific indicators	AR visual positioning	WiFi positioning
Error	MAE(m)	0.854	3.032
	Error extreme(m)	3.175	11.667
	SDE (m)	0.760	2.875
	Cumulative distribution function of the distance errors (CDF)	Shown in analysis	Shown in analysis
Usability	Positioning time (s)	1.30–1.92	1.05–3.35
	Power consumption (Mobile phone)	17%	8%
	System size (MB)	<20	<20
Extensibility	Additional equipment cost (RMB)	0	0
	Mapping time per unit area (s/m^2)	4.36	1.2
Robustness	Error change under light interference	Location failure occurs	No
	Error change under electronic interference	No	Not obvious
Subjective judgement	Difficulty of development	Medium-low	Medium
	Complexity of preprocessing	Low	Low
	Applicable site area	Small & Middle	Large

The multi-dimensional comparison between two methods is shown in Table 3.

In terms of error indicators, AR visual positioning accuracy is higher: Mean absolute error is 0.9 m; Maximum error distance is about 3.2 m, with no obvious abnormal values; Error of the standard deviation is 0.8 m, which indicates that error is less volatile in general; From CDF, 80% of errors are controlled within 1 m and the CDF curve converges to probability of 1.0 faster. In comparison, WiFi positioning accuracy is lower, with mean absolute error at about 3 m. Stability is relatively poor as there is 20% of errors over 3 m and 15% greater than 5 m. Moreover, there shows an 11 m error extremum, indicating a drift phenomenon. The probable reason could be that there exist a few similar fingerprint vectors however spatially apart from each other so that the fingerprint at the user's location might be matched to a fingerprint sample far from the true point in space.

In terms of usability, two methods are similar in results: The initial positioning time of both depends on the speed of map loading from server and the efficiency of localization algorithm, with positioning time cost at 1–2 s; Power consumption and system size of both are on the same level, as WiFi method stores fingerprint as json file and AR visual method saves point cloud as txt file, avoiding large capacity data localized. As stated above, the requirements for mobile devices are quite low.

In view of scalability, both methods don't require additional equipment to achieve localization and WiFi method is three times more efficient. In large-scale scenes, WiFi method has time cost advantage while AR visual method requires specialized equipment, such as panoramic camera assisted, to achieve more convenient and productive locating preparation.

Considering robustness, light has a certain impact to AR visual positioning and thus feature database at daytime cannot be applied at night and vice versa. For WiFi method, as it's hard to control factors including surrounding visitors and electronic devices, its ability to resist environmental interference requires further experiments.

Judgment from the perspective of developers subjectively, preprocessing difficulty of both methods are relatively low. As EasyAR engine has encapsulated some core methods, it's more convenient and slightly easier for developers to realize AR visual positioning than WiFi-based methods.

Overall, the applicability of the two indoor positioning methods to specific scenarios has the following characteristics. WiFi positioning suits for large-scale sites, as the internal differences within fingerprint samples should be as large as possible. With a certain density of AP layout, WiFi fingerprint method can be applied in hospital, major museum, hypermarket, shopping mall and other places. AR visual positioning, in view of its nature of vision, is suitable for rooms, libraries, shopping malls and other scenes with rich texture features and relatively fixed layout. Accuracy may be reduced in scenarios such as supermarket where goods and decorations change frequently. In scenes like office building and teaching building with large areas of white walls and repeated doors and windows, either time cost is increased by collecting feature data in finer details or money cost is added by using expensive equipment like panoramic camera for better mapping.

4 Discussion and Conclusion

In this study, the emerging AR visual positioning method and the widely-used WiFi-based RSS fingerprint positioning method are selected to analyze the characteristics of the two indoor positioning methods from multiple perspectives. The results indicate some commonalities between them: The 3D multi-floor positioning accuracy is rather poor with mapping problem at the connection of stairs between two floors; Usability measures such as positioning time, power consumption and storage space occupation have little difference; No additional equipment is required; Feasibility is heigh as both only require data collection during preprocessing. The main differences between the two methods are as follows: AR visual positioning method is of higher accuracy and stability, and is suitable for indoor environment with rich texture, fixed layout and relatively stable light; Wi-Fi location method is of high volatility with abnormal drift phenomenon now and then, but with higher efficiency in data collection, it has more advantages in usability and is suitable for large-scale location with densely-deployed AP.

The experiments are tried to be conducted under general situation so that the techniques could be duplicated by others to the greatest extent. Besides, many small experiments concerning special condition and different scenarios are considered in this study while there is still much room for progress. Our evaluation methods haven't been tested in other scenarios like markets and hospitals to further solidify the conclusions. Future work will focus on combination of different types of indoor positioning methods, integrating the advantages of emerging technologies and traditional methods. Moreover, different positioning methods should be selected flexibly, aiming at distinctive types of scenarios, so as to improve the accuracy and usability of indoor positioning.

Funding. This work is partially supported by the projects funded by the National Natural Science Foundation of China (Grant Number: 41771410) and the Ministry of Education of China (Grant Number: Ministry of Education of Humanities and Social Science Project 19JZD023).

References

1. Hazas, M., Scott, J., Krumm, J.: Location-aware computing comes of age. Computer **37**(2), 95–97 (2004)
2. Xi, R., Li, Y.J., Hou, M.S.: Survey on indoor localization. Comput. Sci. **43**(4), 1–6+32 (2016)
3. Chen, R.Z., Chen, L.: Indoor positioning with smartphone: the state-of-the-art and the challenges. Acta Geodaetica et Cartographica Sinica **46**(10), 1316–1326 (2017)
4. Li, Q.Q., Zhou, B.D., Ma, W., et al.: Research process of GIS-aided indoor localization. Acta Geodaetica et Cartographica Sinica **48**(12), 1498–1506 (2019)
5. Pei, L., Liu, D.H., Qian, J.C.: A survey of indoor positioning technology and application. Navig. Positioning Timing **4**(03), 1–10 (2017)
6. Chai, P.S.: Indoor positioning and navigation based on mobile devices. East China Normal University (2017)
7. Yan, D.Y., Song, W., Wang, X.D., et al.: Review of development status of indoor location technology in China. J. Navig. Positioning **7**(4), 5–12 (2019)
8. Zhang, N.: Research on image matching algorithm in indoor visual positioning. Shenyang University of Technology (2020)

9. Tao, J.: Research on image matching algorithm in indoor visual positioning. Nanjing University of Posts and Telecommunications (2020)
10. Bahl, P., Padmanabhan, V.N.: RADAR: an in-building RF-based user location and tracking system. In: IEEE Infocom 2000, Tel Aviv, pp. 775–784 (2000)
11. Youssef, M.: Horus: a WLAN-based indoor location determination system. University of Maryland (2004)
12. Xia, S., Liu, Y., Yuan, G., et al.: Indoor fingerprint positioning based on Wi-Fi: an overview. ISPRS Int. J. Geo Inf. **6**(5), 135 (2017)
13. Sivic, J., Zisserman, A.: Video Google: a text retrieval approach to object matching in videos. In: IEEE International Conference on Computer Vision, pp. 1470–1477. IEEE (2003)
14. Lowe, D.G.: Distinctive image features from scale-invariant keypoints. Int. J. Comput. Vis. **60**(2), 91–110 (2004)
15. Bay, H., Tuytelaars, T., Van Gool, L.: Surf: speeded up robust features. In: Leonardis, A., Bischof, H., Pinz, A. (eds.) ECCV 2006. LNCS, vol. 3951, pp. 404–417. Springer, Heidelberg (2006). https://doi.org/10.1007/11744023_32
16. Yu, L.L.: Research on positioning method based on image retrieval. Tianjin University of Technology and Education (2019)
17. Jia, S., Ma, L., Tan, X., et al.: Bag-of-visual words based improved image retrieval algorithm for vision indoor positioning. In: 2020 IEEE 91st Vehicular Technology Conference (VTC2020-Spring), pp. 1–4. IEEE (2020)
18. Yang, Z.: Research and implementation of mobile augmented reality system based on Android platform. Fuzhou University (2018)
19. Gladston, A., Duraisamy, A.: Augmented reality indoor navigation using handheld devices. Int. J. Virtual Augmented Reality (IJVAR) **3**(1), 1–17 (2019)
20. Pang, J., Chen, G.X., Song, G.F., et al.: Research and application of augmented reality map. J. Geomatics **46**(1), 130–134 (2021)
21. Li, M., Chen, R., Liao, X., et al.: A Precise Indoor visual positioning approach using a built image feature database and single user image from smartphone cameras. Remote Sens. **12**(5), 869 (2020)
22. Wu, T., Liu, J., Li, Z., et al.: Accurate smartphone indoor visual positioning based on a high-precision 3D photorealistic map. Sensors **18**(6), 1974 (2018)
23. Yang, S., Ma, L., Jia, S., et al.: An improved vision-based indoor positioning method. IEEE Access **8**, 26941–26949 (2020)
24. Hao, Z., Dang, J., Cai, W., et al.: A multi-floor location method based on multi-sensor and WiFi fingerprint fusion. IEEE Access **8**, 223765–223781 (2020)
25. Bai, W.X.: Research on indoor positioning algorithm based on location fingerprint identification. Lanzhou Jiaotong University (2020)
26. Zhang, R.X.: Research on indoor 3D positioning technology based on WiFi. Nanjing University of Posts and Telecommunications (2018)
27. EasyAR Developer Center (2021). https://www.easyar.com/view/support.html
28. Qin, S.M.: The WiFi indoor location technology based on the fingerprint. University of Electronic Science and Technology of China (2013)
29. Welch, G.: An Introduction to the Kalman Filter. Department of Computer Science, University of North Carolina (2006)
30. GetSensorData. 2.1, July 2019 (2021). https://github.com/lopsi/GetSensorData_Android

Author Index

Printed in the United States
by Baker & Taylor Publisher Services